𝔄 𝔤𝔯𝔞𝔪𝔫

𝔱𝔥𝔢 𝔡𝔦𝔞𝔩𝔢𝔠𝔱 𝔬𝔣

(𝔏𝔞𝔫𝔠𝔞𝔰𝔥𝔦𝔯𝔢)

Karl G. Schilling

Alpha Editions

This edition published in 2019

ISBN : 9789353897895

Design and Setting By
Alpha Editions
email - alphaedis@gmail.com

A GRAMMAR

OF THE

DIALECT OF OLDHAM

(LANCASHIRE).

DISSERTATION

ZUR

ERLANGUNG DER DOKTORWÜRDE

BEI DER

PHILOSOPHISCHEN FAKULTÄT
DER GROSSHERZOGLICH HESSISCHEN LUDWIGS-UNIVERSITÄT
ZU GIESSEN

EINGEREICHT VON

KARL G. SCHILLING
AUS ALTRINCHAM (ENGLAND).

DARMSTADT.
G. OTTO'S HOF-BUCHDRUCKEREI.
1906.

H.

Genehmigt durch das Prüfungskollegium
am 22. I. 1906.
Referent: Dr. Horn.

Preface.

It is intended in the present work to add one more to the list of scientific grammars of English Dialects. The general scheme is the same as that followed by Professor Wright in his Grammar of the Windhill Dialect except that I have, like Hargreaves in his Grammar of the Dialect of Adlington, made Middle English and not Old English the starting point of my investigations. — It is to Professor Horn of Giessen that I am indebted for the idea of writing the grammar as also for his advice and suggestions on every occasion. — I also take this opportunity to thank Mr. Dronsfield of Oldham for his valuable help in the way of practical information concerning the folk-speech of which he is such an admirable exponent.

As the English Dialect Grammar of Dr. J. Wright did not appear until the autumn of 1905, when my grammar was already completed, I was unable to make use of it.

List of Works consulted with Abbreviations used.

Björkman, E. Scandinavian Loanwords in Middle English, Halle 1900—19)2. (Björkman.)

Ellis, A. J. Early English Pronunciation, vol. V, London 1875. (E. E. P.)

Hargreaves, A. A Grammar of the Dialect of Adlington, Heidelberg 1904. (Hargreaves.)

Horn, W. Beiträge zur Geschichte der Gutturallaute, Berlin 1901. (Gutturallaute.)

Horn, W. Untersuchungen zur neuenglischen Lautgeschichte, Strassburg 1905. (= Quellen und Forschungen 98.) (Unters.)

Köppel, E. Spelling Pronunciations, Strassburg 1901. (= Quellen und Forschungen 89.)

Lloyd, R. J. Northern English, Leipzig 1899.

Luick, K. Untersuchungen zur englischen Lautgeschichte, Strassburg 1896. (Unters.)

Murray. New English Dictionary, Oxford. (N. E. D.)

Nodal and Milner. A Glossary of the Lancashire Dialect, Manchester 1875. (Nodal and Milner.)

Sweet, Henry. New English Grammar, Oxford 1892. (N. E. G.)

Taylor, F. E. The Folkspeech of South Lancashire, Manchester 1901. (Taylor.)

Wright, J. A Grammar of the Dialect of Windhill, London 1892.

Wright, J. The English Dialect Dictionary, London 1905. (E. D. D.)

Other Abbreviations.

AFr.	=	Anglo-French (Norman-French).
Fr.	=	French.
Germ.	=	Germanic.
L. (Lat.)	=	Latin.
lit.	=	literary.
LME.	=	Late Middle English.
ME.	=	Middle English.
NE.	=	New (Literary) English.
OD.	=	Oldham Dialect.
OE.	=	Old English.
OFr.	=	Old French.

Misprints.

pp. 89 & 102, read *fornit(š)ə^r* = furniture.

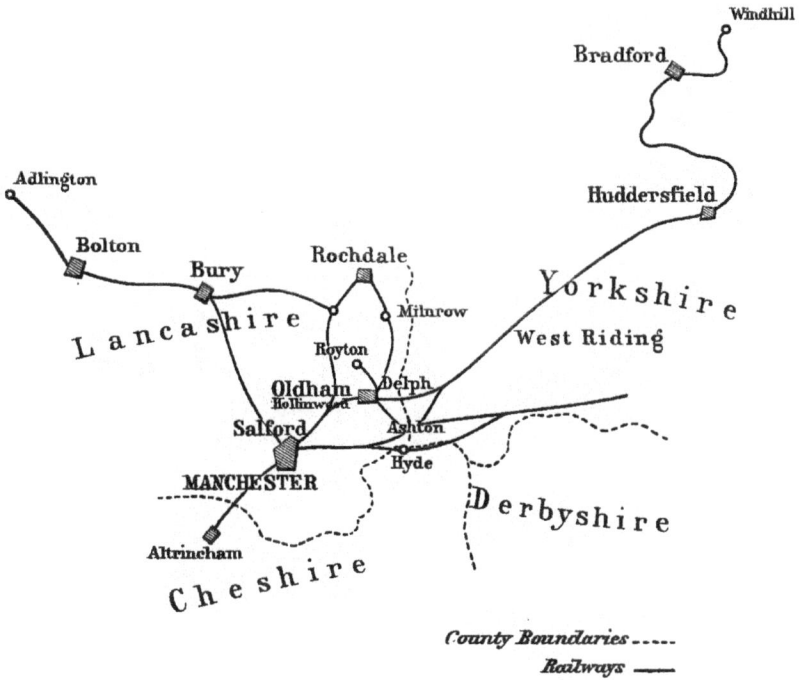

Windhill

Bradford

Huddersfield

Adlington

Bolton

Bury

Rochdale

Milnrow

L a n c a s h i r e

Y o r k s h i r e

West Riding

Royton

Oldham

Hollinwood

Delph

Salford

Ashton

Hyde

MANCHESTER

D e r b y s h i r e

Altrincham

C h e s h i r e

County Boundaries ......
Railways ———

INTRODUCTION.

The Municipal Borough of Oldham, the dialect of which I have attempted in the following pages to discuss, is situated in S. E. Lancashire and therefore falls within District 21 as marked in Ellis' E. E. P., vol V. A glance at the preceding map will show that only a few miles separate it from the adjoining county of Yorkshire (West Riding) the nearest large town in that county being Huddersfield, nor is it far from the N. E. extremity of Cheshire and the N. W. corner of Derbyshire, the strip of land round Staleybridge (Cheshire) being included by Ellis in District 21.

It may be objected that a town so large as Oldham (population over 100,000) is hardly suited for the purpose of showing a distinct variety of dialect in anything like a pure state, but a reference to Ellis (E. E. P., V. p. 322) will show that he has already referred to Oldham as possessing a particular form of speech distinct from the other towns in the immediate neighbourhood.

To say, of course, that the dialect of Oldham is pure would be as untrue as it would be of any other dialect still spoken in Great Britain, but certain causes have worked and are still working which have great influence in preserving the popular speech from too rapid decay. The vast and sudden increase of the population consequent upon the spread of the cotton manufacture at the beginning of last century was certainly a cause for alarm to the lovers of the ancient folk-speech of Lancashire, and it was thought at the time that it would never hold its own against such an invasion

1

of foreign elements, but though a large number of new words were introduced they did not succeed in ousting the native forms, rather the reverse, the foreigners learnt the speech of the natives and became assimilated with them in every way, a process which is still going on in the case of all fresh settlers at the present day. — For this there are particular reasons which I will try to make clear. For the entire district of S. E. Lancashire there is practically only one staple industry, namely that of cotton spinning. Other manufactures are carried on, it is true, but the vast majority of the population is employed in the cotton mills. Moreover not only is male but female labour employed, the cotton operatives are recruited indiscriminately from both sexes. This is very important for the preservation of the dialect, for not only are the male members of the family constantly hearing and speaking the vernacular, but the mothers of the present and future generations also, and no impressions, whether linguistic or otherwise, are so difficult to eradicate as those received in infancy. Add to this that not only are all the foremen in the mills local men who have been bred and born among the dialect-speaking population, but even the wealthy millowners are, as often as not, men who have risen from the ranks and, in every case almost, born in the locality and using the dialect as their habitual medium of conversation. The older generation indeed not only habitually address their hands in the dialect but even speak it among themselves unless strangers are present.

It might be supposed, however, that the spread of education would make itself felt to the detriment of the folk-speech. The younger generation can most of them express themselves in literary English if they choose i. e. at the time at which they leave school to go to the mill, but as they are allowed to work as half-timers between the ages of 12 and 14 (i. e. to spend half the day, either the morning or the afternoon, during these two years in the mill) after which they hear hardly anything but dialect at work and in the home, we cannot wonder at the slow progress made by the literary language in the cotton district.

The present generation of young men and women in Oldham as well as the other manufacturing towns in Lancashire are, it is true, becoming gradually more reticent in the use of the popular speech in the presence of strangers; any attempt, however, to "talk fine", as speaking literary English is called, among themselves is greeted by the older hands as a mark of snobbishness.

Moreover, side by side with this recent gradual extension of the literary language, we have an undercurrent of conservatism in the form of Literary Clubs and Societies whose object it is to preserve the Folk-speech in its pristine vigour. The efforts of these societies are aided by the magnificent library of really first-class dialect literature at their disposal from which to select pieces for public readings or recitals and thus to keep alive the love of the old speech among the people. — Indeed I think I may say without fear of contradiction that there is hardly any corner of Europe which has produced in comparatively recent years such a phalanx of poetry and prose writers in the dialect as S. E. Lancashire. So great, indeed, is the fame of some of them (Edwin Waugh and Ben Brierley for instance) that their works are not only read and enjoyed in their native county but in other parts of England sufficiently remote from the cotton district.

There is yet another factor which tends to preserve the dialects of S. E. Lancashire and that is the exclusiveness of the people. This exclusiveness not only extends to the natives of other counties (notably Yorkshire), but to a less degree, to all strangers not belonging to the same town and village. A man from Oldham will be laughed at in Hollinwood (even tho' the distance between the two places is less than a mile and a continuous street connects them), for the use of certain forms peculiar to his own dialect (*nobət* [Oldham] *nobə*ʳ [Hollinwood] = only [not but]). The same thing is noticeable in Oldham or Rochdale people away from home. They cling together whenever possible and should they come across a fellow-townsman in their travels they hail him with as much effusion as one Frenchman would hail another in a foreign country.

1*

Despite this tenacious clinging to the folk-speech, however, the dialect is undergoing a gradual change more especially in the matter of vocabulary. A mere glance at the very full glossary of South Lancashire words edited by Mr F. E. Taylor (Manchester, 1901) will prove this at once. Mr Taylor has marked the obsolete words with an asterisk and many words so marked are still to be found in the writings of Brierley and Waugh, the latter being barely 50 years old. There are, however, other changes taking place of more vital importance. These affect both vocabulary and phonology. With regard to the former must be mentioned more especially the gradual filtering in of Yorkshire forms, more particularly from the West Riding, as might be expected owing to its proximity to Oldham. Such words I have carefully noted in their proper places. The vocabulary has been, however, much more strongly influenced by the neighbouring Lancashire towns of Rochdale (9 miles from Oldham) and Ashton (about 3 miles away). Among Rochdale words one of the commonest is *wēiš* = "wash" which is found side by side with the Oldham *weš* (*waš*). Among Ashton words is a whole group, namely those ending in the literary language in -*ing* which in the Oldham dialect all appear without a final *ŋ*-sound (e. g. *šilin* = 'shilling' &c), but in Ashton have changed *ŋ* into *ŋk* (e. g. *šiliŋk*).

Between the dialect of Oldham proper and that of the outlying villages which the growing town is gradually absorbing there is, of course, a process of assimilation going on, one or more variants of the same word being often found side by side. Another factor tending to the mixture of the dialects is the spread of dialect literature from one Lancashire town to another. This literature mostly takes the form of little penny books in the vernacular which are eagerly bought and read by the mill-hands. In this manner a large number of Bolton words have found their way into the Rochdale and Oldham dialects despite the fact that Bolton is the centre of a colliery district and that the colliers and the mill-hands have little intercourse in the ordinary way. Perhaps it will cause surprise to those unacquainted with the locality to hear that despite the proximity of Manchester (the distance between Oldham and Manchester is only 6 miles), the Oldham dialect has been hardly effected at all by the neighbourhood of the great city. The mill-hands employed in the Manchester cotton mills are drawn from a large number of neighbouring cotton towns and form a very unstable part of the population, constantly coming and going.

Moreover the mill-owners of Manchester live far out in the suburbs and do not come into contact with their hands nearly so often as those living in Oldham and the smaller cotton towns, so that one of the chief factors for the preservation of a strong and healtly dialect is missing.

Phonologically the most noticeable recent change is perhaps the new pronunciation of such literary English words as *there*, *where*, *stairs* &c, which should be pronounced in the pure dialect as *ðiəʳ*, *wiəʳ*, *stiəʳz* but are now often heard as *ðɛʳ*, *wɛʳ*, *stɛ̄ɾz*. Mere weak sentence stress will not explain this pronunciation as it is extended to words (such as *stɛ̄ʳz*) which could hardly be weakly stressed under any circumstances.

There now remains to consider the composition of the vocabulary of the Oldham Dialect from the etymological point of view. Few words will suffice here. The vast majority of the words is, as might be supposed, of English origin. The Scandinavian element is not nearly so important as in the neighbouring dialects of Yorkshire where many Scandinavian forms have survived owing to the long Danish settlement. The Celtic element is a little more noticeable in Lancashire than in Yorkshire but, as in the rest of England proper, forms only a very small item in the vocabulary. The French element consists mostly of such words as are found in Middle English, tho' a few have crept in later under the influence of the literary language.

PART I

PHONOLOGY.

CHAPTER I

SOUNDS OF THE DIALECT.

I. THE VOWELS.

§ 1. The Oldham Dialect contains the following vowels:

a) Short Vowels: *a, e, i, o, u, ṵ, ə.*

b) Long Vowels: *ā, ẹ̄, ī, ǭ, ọ̄, ū, ə̄.*

c) Diphthongs: *ai, ẹ̄i, īə, au, ūə, ęu.*
əi, ēə, oi, ọ̄ə, ui, ié.

A short description of the Oldham Vowels follows. ę ǫ represent the spen sounds, ẹ, ọ respresent the closed sounds.

a) Short Vowels.

a (mid-back-wide) like *a* in German "Mann", e. g. *lad* = lad, *arə* = arrow, *brast* = burst, *watš* = watch.

e (mid-front-wide) as in standard English *men, help* &c., e. g. *neb* = peak of a man's cap, *neš* = tender, *wentš* = a girl.

i (high-front-wide) as in standard English *bit*, e. g. *brid* = brid, *sitš* = such, *sikst* = sixth.

o (mid-back-wide-round) like *o* in the German „Stock“, e. g. *frozn* = frozen, *mony* = many.

u (high-back-wide-round) like in standard English *put*, e. g. *puns* = to kick, *þunə^r* = thunder.

ų. This is the same sound as Hargreaves denotes by the symbol. It comes nearer o than *u* (cp. Hargreaves p. 4), e. g. *kųm* = come, *wųs* = worse.

ə (mid-mixed-narrow) as *e* in German „Gabe", e. g. *arə* = arrow, *ōləz* = always, *nētďə^r* = nature.

b) Long Vowels.

ā (mid-back-wide) like *a* in German "Haar" occurs mostly before *^{r}*, e. g. *ām* = to mock, *a^{r}k* = chest, *āsk* = a water-newt.

Note: Hargreaves gives this *ā* before *^{r}* the value "ä" and his *ā* as only occurring where we have *əi* in the Oldham Dialect.

ẹ̄ (mid-front-narrow) as in German "See", e. g. *fẹ̄b^{r}i* = gooseberry, *gẹ̄t* = road, way, *lẹ̄ik* = to play.

ī (high-front-narrow) like the *i* in German "Biene", e. g. *drī* = tedious, *grīt* = to cry, *nīt* = night.

ǭ (low-back-narrow-round) as *aw* in standard English "*saw*", e. g. *kǭv* = calf, *fǭs* = cunning, *ǭf* = elf, idiot.

ọ̄) mid-back-narrow-round) like German "so", e. g. *bọ̄* = ball, *krọ̄p* = crept, *lọ̄p* = leapt.

ū (high-back-narrow-round) like *u* in German "du", e. g. *əbūn* = above, more than, *brū* = hill, *fū* = fool.

ā̃ (low-back-narrow), e. g. *kā̃^{r}sn* = to christen, *wā̃'tš* = to work, *jā̃^{r}þ-bobz* = tufts of heather.

c) Diphthongs

ai = *a* + *ī*. The *i* is high-front-narrow and is long. In the Oldham Dialect there are many words where the vowel sound fluctuates between *ai* and *əi*. In the following the *ai* sound is the more common: *abaid* = to suffer, *flait* = to scold, quarrel, *naifl* = a delicacy, *paik* = to pick, choose.

ei = *e* + *ī*. As above the *i* is high-front-narrow and is long, e. g. *feit* = fight, *fleiš* = flesh, *weiš* (or *weš*) = waah.

īə, e. g. *əfīə′t* = afraid, *bīəs* = beasts, *pīə′tš* = perch.

au. This sound (or the nearest approximation to it) is represented by Hargreaves as *ou*. He says it is a more open sound than Sweet's *ou* and lies between his *ou* + *au*. In the O. D. it lies distinctly nearer *au*, e. g. *aud* = old, *kaud* = cold, *haud* = hold, *maudiwō′p* = mole.

ŭə, e. g. *duə′* = door, *əfuə′* = before, *muə′* = more, *kuəl (kwʊt)* = coat.

ęu, e. g. *ręund* = round, *bęut* = without, *ęuə′* = our, *teun* = town.

Note: In neighbouring dialects this *ęu* appears as *ā*.

ę̄ə, e. g. *bę̄ə′* = bear, *swę̄ə′* = swear.

oi, e. g. *əpoint* = appoint, *loin* = loin, *soil* = soil.

Q̄ə, e. g. *bifQ̄ə′* = before, *fQ̄ə′* = four.

ui, e. g. *ruin* = ruin, *suit* = suet.

ié. It only occurs in the word *þiétə′* = theatre.

əi has the same sound as the French *eui* in *feuille*, e. g. *bəil* = boil, *wəild* = wild, *tšəild* = child.

II. THE CONSONANTS.

§ 2. The Oldham Dialect contains the following consonants: *b, d, f, g, j, k, l, m, n, ŋ, p, r, s, š, t, þ, đ, v, w, z, ž.*

b (lip-stop-voice). It occurs initially, medially and finally, e. g. *blud* = blood, *abit* = habit, *rub* = rub.

d (gum-stop-voice). It occurs in all positions, e. g. *dautə′* = daughter, *medsin* = medicine, *kaud* = cold.

Note: Hargreaves has also a symbol *ḍ* to represent the sound of *d* before *r* or in a syllable containing *r*. In the Oldham Dialect this *ḍ* is unnecessary, as under the circumstances *d* becomes either *dđ* or, more commonly *d*.

f (lip-teeth-open-breath). It occurs in all positions, e. g. *fəind* find, *ofə′* = offer, *wəif* = wife.

g (back-stop-voice). It occurs in all positions, e. g. *gam* = fun, *figə′* = figure, *leg* = leg.

j (front-open-voice) like lit. Engl. *y* in *you*. It only occurs initially, e. g. *jalə* = yellow, *jit* = yet.

Note: The glide sound of *j* mentioned by Hargreaves as occurring occasionally in the Adlington Dialect is not found in the Oldham Dialect *k* (back-stop-breath). It occurs in all positions, e. g. *kaud* = cold, *akə* = acre, *tak* = take.

l (gum-side-voice) resembling a German l more than a London English one. It occurs in all positions, but is syllabic only in unaccented syllables, e. g. *levl* = level, *luv* = love, *milk* = milk, *kil* = kill. Of these the second *l* in *levl* is syllabic.

m (lip-nasal-voice), e. g. *mon* = man, *simpl* = simple, *kṵm* = come.

n (gum-nasal-voice). It occurs in all positions, e. g.: *nīdl* = needle, *untə* = hunter, *brazen* = brazen, impertinent. Vocalic *n* occurs in unaccented syllables only (mostly finally), e. g. *brazn* = brazen, *frozn* = frozen, *brokn* = broken.

ŋ (back-nasal-voice). It is only found in the combinations *ŋg* and *ŋk* when it has the same value as lit. Engl. *ng* and *nk* (in Finger), e. g. *siŋg* = sing, *stiŋk* = stink.

p (lip-stop-breath). It occurs initially, medially and finally, e. g. *peund* = pound, *api* = happy, *lomp* = lamp.

r. This sound is described by Hargreaves as gum-open-voice. Initially and medially between vowels it has the same sound as lit. Engl. *r* in the same position; finally, or medially the preceding vowel becomes what is described by Lloyd as "coronal vowel" [cp. Lloyd's "Northern English" § 100 ff.], e. g. *reum* = room, *krīp* = creep, *beri* = berry, *kə̄s* = curse, *swiə* = swear. In the last two examples the vowel is "coronal".

s (blade-open-breath) like *s* in lit. Engl. *sit*. It occurs in all positions, e. g. *sārtin* = certain, *bēsn* = basin, *šips* = ships.

š (blade-point-open-breath) like lit. Engl. *sh* in *shall*. It occurs in all positions, e. g. *šadə* = shadow, *bušl* = bushel, *fīš* = fish

t (gum-stop-breath). It occurs in all positions, e. g. *teum* = town, *batl* = battle, *fəit* = fight.

Note: Hargreaves has also a symbol *ţ* but like his *ḍ* it is not necessary in the Oldham dialect being perfally well represented either by *td̄* or *þ*.

þ (teeth-open-breath) like *th* in lit. Engl. *thick*. It occurs in all positions, e. g. *þunə^r* = thunder, *elþi* = healthy, *meuþ* = mouth.

đ (teeth-open-voice) like *th* in lit. Engl. *this*. It occurs in all positions, e. g. *đis* = this, *fa^rđin* = farthing, *brīđ* = breathe.

v (lip-teeth-open voice) like the *v* in lit. Eng. *vane*. It occurs in all positions, e. g. *veri* = very, *waivz (wəivz)* = wives, *luv* = love.

w (lip-back-open-voice) like Engl. *w* in *water*. It occurs initially and medially, e. g. *wəin* = wine, *wīš* = wish, *əwēⁱ* = away.

z (blade-open-voice) like lit. Engl. *z* in *freeze*. It is rare initially, commoner medially and finally, e. g. *zeundz!* = zounds!, *jezi* = easy, *tšīz* = cheese.

ž (blade-point-open-voice) like lit. Engl. *s* in *pleasure*. It mostly occurs in combination with *d* as *dž*, e. g. *džəin* = join, *indžin* = engine, *edž* = edge.

Note: Hargreaves has also a sound *ʒ* (p. 7) but in the Oldham Dialect it is indistinguishable from final *z*.

THE SOUNDS TREATED HISTORICALLY.

CHAPTER II.

THE VOWELS IN ACCENTED SYLLABLES.

SECTION I.

THE VOWELS CONSIDERED SINGLY.

SHORT VOWELS.

a.

1. Spontaneous Development.

A. English Sources.

§ 3.

1. ME. *a* appears in the Oldham Dialect as *a*.

a) From OE. *a, æ, ea*:

1) From OE. *a*:

ME.	OD.	NE.
ankel	*aŋkel*	ankle
arwe	*arə*	arrow
ax(e)	*aks*	axe
bannen	*ban*	to curse
castél	*kasl*	castle
crabbe	*krab*	crab
krakien	*krak*	a gossiping conversation
fan	*fan*	fan
gamen	*gam*	game.

2) From OE. *ae*:

ME.	OD.	NE.
akern	*atšə̆ʳn*	acorn
after	*afdəʳ*	after
bath	*baþ*	bath
blak	*blak*	black
bras	*bras*	brass, money
barst, brast	*brast*	burst
bac	*bak*	back
cappe	*kap*	cap
daft	*daft*	silly
fast	*fast*	fast
hat	*at*	hat

ME.	OD.	NE.		ME.	OD.	NE.
lappe	*lap*	lap (sb)		c) ME. *a* from OE. *æ*:		
masse	*mas*	mass				
mast	*mast*	mast		ani	*ani*	any
rafter	*rafđər*	rafter		fat(t)	*fat*	fat
				laddre	*ladđər*	ladder

3) From OE. *ea*:

galwes	*galəsis*	braces
narowe ⎱ narwe ⎰	*nurə*	narrow

laste	*last*	last (sb)
mad	*mad*	mad

b) ME. *a* from OE. *ā*:

ascen, axen	*ax*	to ask
attercoppe	*atđərkrop*	spider
(y)clad	*klad*	clad
lammasse	*laməs*	lammas

d) ME. *a* from OE. *ēa*:

chapman	*tšap*	chap
	tšapmon	a purchaser
chaffare	*tšafər*	to haggle
laþer	*ladər* (*lođər*)	lather

B. Scandinavian Sources.

ME. *a* from. Scandinavian *a* (*o*):

farand	*farant(li)*	hand-somely
gabbe	*gab*	impudence
gad	*gad*	loiter
haplice	*aplinz*	haply

cratchinge	*kratšinz*	refuse of melted lead
cang	*kaŋk* (*koŋk*)	a grossiping conversation
clacke	*klak*	chatter
ragge	*rag*	rag

C. Celtic Sources.

ME. *a* from Celtic *a*:

brat	*brat*	coarse apron

cammid	*kamd*	cross-tempered
ladde	*lad*	lad
lasse	*las*	lass.

D. French Sources.

ME. *a* < French *a* (*ā*).

a) French *a* in open syllables unaccented in O. F.

banere	*banər*	banner
barel	*barel*	barrel
bataille	*bat(e)l*	battle
carry	*kari*	kari
damage	*damidž*	damage
favour	*favər*	toresemble

gallon	*galən*	gallon
parische	*pariš*	parish
valeie ⎱ value ⎰	*vali*	⎰ valley ⎱ value

b) French *a* (*ā*) in closed syllables unaccented in O. F.

cacchen	*katš*	catch
champion	⎰ *tšampjən* ⎱ *tšompjən*	champion

ME.	OD.	NE.	ME.	OD.	NE.
fasoun	*fašn*	fashion	mantel	*mantl* }	mantle
lanterne	*lanþəʳn*	lantern		*manti* }	
			passion	*pašn*	passion.

E. Uncertain Sources.

dab	*dab*	a blow	baðen	*baþ*	bathe
crank	*kraŋki*	{ mentally deranged	brasen	*brazn*	impudent
band	*bant*	string.	hasel	*hazl*	hazel
			maken	*mak*	make
Note: OE. and OFr. *a* (*œ, ea*)			schame	*šam*	shame
have not been lengthened in the			taken	*tak*	take
following:			waken	*waken*	waken
			favour	*favəʳ*	to resemble
aker	*akəʳ*	acre	labo(u)r	*labəʳ*	labour
babi	*babi*	babi	naperōn	*apəʳn*	apron
baken	*bak*	bake	paper	*papəʳ*	paper.

2. Development in Combination.

§ 4.

1) ME. *a* + (NE.) final *l* = *ǭ*.

al	*ǭ*	all
al + rẹ̄di	*ǭredi*	already
alweies	*ǭlez*	always
bal	*bǭ*	ball
callen	*kǭ*	call
fallen	*fǭ*	fall
smal	*smǭ*	small.

Note: The above also occur with *ǭ*.

2) *a* + *l* before *f, m, k, s, t* = *ǭ*.

alf	*ǭf*	elf
calf	*kǭv*	calf
half	*ǭv (ǭf)*[1]	half.
halm	*(h)ǭm*	handle of an axe
palm	*pǭm*	palm

balk	*bǭk*	a log of timber
calke	*kǭkəʳz*	turned down portions of a horseshoe
talk-en	*tǭk*	talk
fals	*fǭs*	sly. cunning
faltren	*fǭtəʳ*	to falter
halter	*(h)ǭtəʳ*	halter
malt	*mǭt*	malt
salt	*sǭt*	salt
walten	*wǭt*	to upset.

3) ME. *a* (*o*) before *m, n, ŋ* = *o* except when *w* precedes.

bank	*boŋk*	bank
cang	*koŋk*	a gossiping conversation

---

[1] The Rochdale form *ēf* is also heard, cp also Hargreaves, p. 26, 30, and Horn, Untersuchungen p. 18.

ME.	OD.	NE.	ME.	OD.	NE.
cann	*kon*	can	slaschen	*slaiš*	slash
conny	*koni*	brave, fine	?	*smaiš*[1]	smash
candel	*kondel*	candle	wasshe	*waiš*	wash.
chance (chaunce)	*tsons*	chance		(*weš*)[2]	
gander	*gonər* (*gondər*)	gander			
grand	*gron(d)*	grand			
grant (graunt)	*gront*	grant			
hamme	*om*	ham			
hamer	*omər*	hammer			
hamme + schaklin	*omšakl*	to hinder			
hand	*ond (ont)*	hand			
man	*mon*	man			
mani	*moni*	many			
planke	*ploŋk*	plank			
ram	*rom*	ram			
ranc	*roŋk*	rank			
spannen	*spon*	span			
standen	*stond*	stand			
trampelen	*trompl*	trample.			

Note: ME. *asche* (pl. asches) has not become *aiš* as might be expected, but *es*.

5) ME. *a* + final *r* = *ər*.

ME.	OD.	NE.
dar	*dər*	dare
far	*fər*	far
gar-en	*gər*	to force, compel
war(re)	*wər*	worse.

Note 1: *w* + ME. *a* = *wa* except before *l* + consonant.

swan	*swan*	swan
wace	*waken*	waken
wacche	*watš*	watch
war	*war*	war
warm	*warm*	warm.

Note 2: ME. *a* + final *s* has sometimes become *ā*, but only in certain words e. g. *dlās* = glass, *lās* = lass, *ās* = ass. But these words are also found with *ă*.

4) ME *a* + *š* = *aiš*.

dasshe	*daiš*	dash
lasshe	*laiš*	lash
paschen	*paiš*	to pour down
rasshe	*raiš*	rash

[1] Skeat "Etymological Dictionary" derives this word from a doubtful Swedish Dialect word *smacke*.

[2] The Rochdale form *weiš* (ex ME. *wesschen*?) is also found.

e.

1. Spontaneous Development.

A. English Sources.

§ 5.

ME. *e* (from OE. *e, eo*) mostly appears as *e* in the Oldham Dialect.

ME.	OD.	NE.
	belđǝ^r *belder*	to cry out
betere	*betđǝ^r*	better
clemmen	*klem*	to starve
delf	*delf*	a stone quarry
delfen	*delv.*	to dig
O. E. edisc	*ediš* *editš*	second crop of meadow grass
O. E. exen	*exen*	oxen
ellerne ellarne	*eller*	alder-tree
fremede	*frem*	not akim
helfe	*elv*	handle of a spade
kempe	*kempi*	a man fond of fighting
léke	*lek*	to leak
leng(er)	*leŋgǝ^r*	longer
neb	*neb*	peak of a man's cap
nesshe	*neš*	tender, delicate
weft	*weft*	anything woven
welden	*weld*	to wield
wellen	*wel*	to boil
wenchel	*wentš*	a girl.

B. Scandinavian Sources.

ME. *e* = Scandinavian *e*:

ME.	OD.	NE.
degen	*dek* *deg*	to sprinkle / to cut off
eggen	*eg-on*	to incite
felawe	*feli*	fellow
helder	*eldǝ^r* *elđǝ^r*	rather.

C. French Sources.

a) ME. *e* = French *ẹ, ẹ ē* (accented):

ar(r)este	*arest*	arrest
comence	*komens*	commence
defenden	*difend*	defend
effect	*ifekt*	effect
excepcioun	*eksepšǝn*	exception
election	*lekšǝn*	election
fente	*fent*	remnant of cloth
tenten	*tenter*	minder (in a mill).

b) ME. *e* = French *ẹ, ẹ ē* (secondary accent):

aventure	*ventđǝ^r*	venture
beverage	*bebridz*	beverage

ME.	OD.	NE.	ME.	OD.	NE.
medlen ⎱ mellen ⎰	*mel*	to meddle	neveu	*nevi*	nephew
merril	*meril*	a game	trestel	*trest*	a large stool

D. Unknown Sources.

elsin	*elsin*	awl	heter	*hetə*ʳ	keen, eager
		Sb. condition	(quick,		(of dogs)
fetten		⎱	rough)	.	
(make ready)	*fettle*	⎰ Vb. to mend	kebben (to contend)	*keb*	to lean against
flecked	*flekt*	spotted	plecke	*plek*	place
gesc	*ge̊š*	guess	slede	*sled*	sledge
(N. E D.)			snekke	*snek*	latch of door
			tenten	*tent*	stretch.

2. Development in Combination.

§ 6.

1. ME. e + r = ə̄ʳ, ə̄ʳ, ā̄ʳ.

a) ə̄ʳ:

berme	*bə̄ʳm*	barm
cerren	*kə̄ʳn*	churn
dernen	*də̄ʳn*	to darn
ernest	*jə̄ʳnest (jā̄ʳnest)* ⎱	earnest
hert	*hə̄ʳt*	heart
hweþer	*hwə̄ʳ*	whether
kerven	*kə̄ʳv (kā̄ʳv)* ⎱	carve
nerre	*nə̄ʳ*	nearer.

b) ə̄ʳ:

gers	*gə̄ʳs*	grass
gert	*gə̄ʳt*	girt
herce	*hə̄ʳst jə̄ʳst* ⎱	hearse
perken	*pə̄ʳk*	perch
terrible	*tə̄rəbl*	terrible.

c) ā̄ʳ:

1. English Words.

bere-tun	*bā̄ʳten*	barn
derk	*dā̄ʳk*	blind
ernest	*jā̄ʳnest (jə̄ʳnest)*	earnest
herre	*hā̄ʳ*	higher
herke	*hā̄ʳk*	to listen
ker	*kā̄ʳ*	low-lying marsh
kerven	*kā̄ʳv(kə̄ʳv)*	carve
lernen	*lā̄ʳn*	learn, teach
serke	*sā̄ʳk*	shirt
sker	*skā̄ʳ*	a rocky place
sterten	*stā̄ʳt*	start
sterven	*stā̄ʳv*	starve
þerf	*þā̄ʳf (-kēk)* ⎱	cake of oatmeal, butter and treacle
werk	*wā̄ʳk*	work (Subst.)
werlde	*wā̄ʳld*	world.

2. French Words.

ME.	OD.	NE.
certain	sắrtin	certain
concern	konsắrn	concern
conversen	konvắrs	converse
converten	konvắrt	convert
desert	dizắrt	desert
deserven	dizắrv	deserve
determinc	ditắrmin	determine
diversion	divắršən	diversion
merci	mắrsi	mercy
merchant(a)	mắrtšənt	merchant
merveil	mắrvil	marvel
nerfe	nắrvz	nerves
preservcn	prisắrv	preserve
serche	sắrts	search
sermon	sắrmən	sermon
serpent	sắrpənt	serpent
servant	sắrvənt	servant
serven	sắrv	serve.

2. ME. *e* sometimes appears as *ēi* before *š*, but this is an importation from the neighbouring dialect of Rochdale, cp. Hargreaves p. 29. 3. a, b.

ME.	OD.	NE.
flesc	flēiš [flaiš]	flesh, meat
nesshe	nēiš [neš]	tender
weschen	wēiš[waiš, weš]	wash

Note: The OE. word "Grendel" of "Beowulf" is still met in the Lancashire Dialects (including Oldham) = a waterdemon to frighten children. It appears in the form Grindylow (grindilau), cp. F. E. Taylor "Folkspeech of S. Lancs" and Nodal and Milner "Glossary of the Lanc. Dialect" p. 169.

i.

1. Spontaneous Development.

A. English Sources.

§ 7.

ME. *i* usually appears as *i*.

a) ME. *i* = OE. *i*.

ME.	OD.	NE.
blind	blint	blind
brid	brid	bird
brinnen	brindl (up)	to fly into a passion
child	tšilt [tšəilt]	child
cribbe	krib	pinfold
cwic	wik	alive, lively
drifen	driv [druv, ðruv]	driven
finne	finz	fish-bones
gilte	gilt	young female pig
innewarde	inərdz	interior parts
kist	kist	chest
liggen	lig	lie down
likli	likli	likely

2

ME.	OD.	NE.
michel	*mitš*	much
sib	*sib*	akin
singen	*siŋg*	a musical festival
sixte	*sikst*	sixth
spitel	*spitl*	a baker's shovel
siþen	*sin*	since
slinken	*sliŋk*	diseased meat
slideren	*slidər*	slide
twinling	*twindlin*	a twin
þridde	*þrid*	third
wimplen	*wimpl*	to ripple as a brook
windwunge	*winrọ̈* *windrọ̈*	hay put together before housing
windelstrē	*windelstrē*	coarse grass
winter	*winþər*	winter
widi	*widənz*	osiers, willows

b) ME. *i* = OE. *y*.

ME.	OD.	NE.
briğge	*bridž*	bridge
bisi	*bizi*	busy
chist	*tšist*	chest
dine	*din*	noise
dide	*did*	did
kilne	*kil*	kiln
kissen	*kis*	kiss (vb.)
micele	*mikel*	size, bulk
miche	*mitš*	much
milne	*mil*	mill
rigge	*ridžər*	part of harness
rinele	*rindl*	a channel
rippen	*ripər*	a reckless fellow
OE. pl. ge-scyldru[1]	*šildər* *šildər* (*šūdə̆ʳ*)	shoulder
swich	*sitš*	such
(þinchen)	*þiŋk*	think
trindil	*trindl*	wheel of a wheel-barrow.

B. Scandinavian Sources.

ME.	OD.	NE.
biggen	*big*	to build
biker	*bikər*	small wooden tub
blinken	*bliŋkərt*	blind of one eye
clinken	*kliŋk*	a blow
dillen	*dil*	to lull
fisken+gig	*fizgig*	a flirting girl
flinder	*flindərz* *flindərz*	fragments
gildre	*gildərz* *gilerz*	twisted hair for fishing lines
griskin	*griškin*	loin of pork
gimbire	*gimər*	young female sheep
giglot	*giglət*	a wanton girl
impen	*imp*	to rob
kippen	*kipər*	amorons
lic-	*likər*	more likely
ling	*liŋg*	cut and dried heather
(nigard)	*nigl*	to trifle haggle
schift	*šift*	to move, remove
skift	*skift*	
riften	*rift*	to belch
riven	*rivn*	rent, ill-tempered
smiđđe	*smidi*	smithy
spink	*spiŋk*	chaffinch

[1] Cp. Anglia-Beiblatt XVI, 332.

ME.	OD.	NE.	ME.	OD.	NE.
tippen	*tip, tipl*	to upset	wimbil	*wimbl*	quick,lively
tit	*tit(ə͏ʳ)*	soon(er)	wikir	*wikən*	{ mountain ash.

C. French Sources.

ME. *i* = Fr. *i*, *ĭ* (Principal or Secondary Accent).

gilofre	*dźilivə͏ʳ*	gilly-flower	prime + rose	*primrōz*	primrose
gimelot	*gimblət*	gimlet	riban	*ribin*	ribbon
gingebreed	*dźĭndĕ-bred*	ginger-bread	sillable	*sinəbl*	syllable
nifle	*nifl*	to be fas-tidions	simple	*simpl*	simple, humble
pikin	*pik*	to push sharply	sisoures	*siðə͏ʳz*	scissors
			wisard	*wizə͏ʳt*	wizard
pismire	*pisəmūe͏ʳ*	ant	ficche	*fitš*	vetch.
pissen +	*pis-ə-bed*	dandelion			

ME. *i* > **OD.** *e.*

sirupe	*serəp*	syrup
spirit	*sperit*	spirit.

D. ME. *i* from other Teutonic Sources.

cbitte	*tšit*	a pert girl	hipping	*(h)ipiŋ-stüənz*	stepping-stones
crinklen	*kriŋkl*	to crease			
drifte	*drift*	drove of cattle	kitelen	*kitl*	ticklish
			lift	*lift*	left (opp. of "right")
glistren	*glistə͏ʳ*	to shine			
grippen	*gripn*	clasped hands	sissen	*siz*	to hiss.

E. Uncertain Sources.

crikke	*krik*	a painful strain	tikelen	*tik*	to touch
			titten	*tiðə͏ʳ-up*	rouse up
digge	*dig*	duck	twiteren	*twitə͏ʳ*	to tremble
gingelinge	*dźiŋgəlz*	St. Antho-ny's fire	þrimlen	*þrimbl*	to tremble
			þwitel	*þwitl*	a large knife
grig	*grig*	a cricket			
nippe	*nip*	to snatch	wippen +	*(h)wip-stä͏ʳt*	an upstart
sind	*sind*	to rince in water	wisk	*(h)wisk-telt*	wanton
snizen	*snidž*	to curry favour	wiđer	*wiðə͏ʳ*	strong, lusty.
tikel	*tikəl*	fastidious			

2*

2. Development in Combination.

§ 8.

1. ME. i ($\ddot{u}$) before r = a) $\ddot{\partial}^r$ in closed syllables.

ME.	OD.	NE.
bir (bür)	$b\ddot{\partial}^r$	velocity, force
birlen	$b\ddot{\partial}^r l$	to pour out
firre + bobbe	$f\ddot{\partial}^r bobs$	fir-cones
hirte	$\ddot{\partial}^r t$	hurt
hwirl	$w\ddot{\partial}^r(l)$	velocity
mirþren	$m\ddot{\partial}^r d\partial^r$ $m\ddot{\partial}^r d\partial^r$ }	murder
pirge	$p\ddot{\partial}^r d\check{z}$	purge
schirte	$\check{s}\ddot{\partial}^r t$	shirt
stirien	$st\ddot{\partial}^r$	stir
stirke	$st\ddot{\partial}^r k$ {	one-year-old heifer
wirchen	$w\ddot{\partial}^r t\check{s}$	work (vb.)
wirm	$w\ddot{\partial}^r m$	worm.

b) = OD. er in open syllables.

birrien	$beri$	bury
miracle	$mer\partial k\partial l$	miracle
mirie	$meri$	merry
spirit	$sperit$	spirit
(wirwen)	$werit$ ($w\partial rit$)	worry.

ME.	OD.	NE.
c) = OD. $\bar{a}^r$ (Rare).		
kirnel	$k\bar{a}^r n\partial l$	kernel
þirde	$þ\bar{a}^r d$	third
þirtig	$þ\bar{a}^r ti$	thirty.

2. ME. $i + gh$ (χ) before $t = \bar{\imath}$.

bright	$br\bar{\imath}t$	bright
frighten	$fr\bar{\imath}tn$	frighten
lighten	$l\bar{\imath}t(\partial)nin$	lightning
night	$n\bar{\imath}t$	night
right	$r\bar{\imath}t$	right
sight	$s\bar{\imath}t$	sight.

Note: An apparent exception is formed by the form $f\bar{e}it$ = to fight, but this is probably not derived from ME. *fight*, but *feht*.

3. ME. $i + \check{s} = \bar{\imath}\check{s}$.

disshe	$d\bar{\imath}\check{s}$	dish
fisch	$f\bar{\imath}\check{s}$	fish
wisshen	$w\bar{\imath}\check{s}$	wish.

4. ME. i (y) = u in the following:

firste	$f\under{u}st$ ($fost$)	first
schytel	$\check{s}\underline{u}tl$	shuttle.

O.

1. Spontaneous Development.

A. English Sources.

§ 9.

ME. *o* usually remains *o* in the OD.

a) ME. *o* = OE. *o*.

ME.	OD.	NE.
boþem	*boþem*	bottom
brok	*brok*	a badger
brosten	*brosn*	burst
chosen	*tšozn*	chosen
clokken	*klok*	to cluck
clomb-en	*klom*	climbed [pret. and p. pl.]
cloven	*klovn*	cloven
coc?	*kokit*	au impudent girl
cod?(NED.)	*kod*	to banter
cop?(NED.)	*kop*	to catch hold

ME.	OD.	NE.
coper	*kopə^r*	copper
croft	*kroft*	field
crop	*krop*	stomach
folc	*fok*	folk
folȝen	*folə^r*	to follow
foreward	*forəd*	forward
frogge	*frog*	frog
mot	*mot*	a mark to aim at
openen	*op(ə)n*	open
rop	*rops*	intestines
schonke	*šoŋks*	shanks
þrostle	*þrosl*	thrush.

b) ME. *o* = OE. *e*.

focchen	*fotš*	to fetcb.

c) ME. *o* = OE. *eo*.

ȝond	*jon(d)*	yonder.

B. Scandinavian Sources.

blot	*blotš*	a blot
bobbin	*bobin*	a reel
colop	*koləp*	rasher of bacon
doze	*dozənin*	dozing
fon	*fond*	foolish
glopnen	*glopn*	to astonish

odde	*od*	to make equal
offal	*ofəl*	internal parts
roggen	*rog*	to rattle
scoperell	*skopəril*	a spinning top.

C. Other Teutonic Sources.

blobure	*blob*	to bubble
clodde	*clod*	a grass turf
cnokil	*nokəlz*	knuckles
lollen?	*lolopin*	awkward
lompe	*lomper*	to walk clumsily

moppe	*mopit*	a pert girl
soppe	*sop*	to soak
toteren	*todl*	to walk
trollin	*trol*	a loose woman.

D. French Sources.

a) ME. *o* = Fr. *ǫ*, (*o*) (accented).

ME.	OD.	NE.
comicalle	*komikil*	comical
hobeler	*hobil*	a block head
jobarde	*džobə'*	a foolish
	-naul	fellow
provende	*provn*	provender
roket	*rokit*	an outer garment
volume	*voləm*	volume.

b) ME. *o* = Fr. *ǫ*, (*o*) (unaccented).

ME.	OD.	NE.
conceit	*konsēt*	conceit
converten	*konvā'rt*	convert
gob	*gob*	mouth
loggen	*lodž*	a reservoir
ossen	*os*	to try
poshot	*posət*	posset

E. Celtic Sources.

bobbe	*bob*	to dance about
boglen	*bogl*	to hesitate be afraid
fogge	*fog*	grass after mowing
jobbin	*job*	to stab
scrog	*skrog*	a fragment.

F. ME. *o* from Unknown Sources.

brodden (?)	*brodl*	to swagger
colok	*kolok*	a large pail
costrelle	*kostril*	a little barrel
hoppere	*opə'r*	sort of basket
lopren	*lopə'rt*	curdled
schocken (?)	*šog*	to jog.

2. Development in Combination.

§ 10.

1. ME. *o* has two developments before *r*.

a) = *ǫr*.

corde	*kwǭrd*	cord
forʒifen	*fǭ'gén*	forgiven
fortune	*fǭ'rtin*	fortune
	(*fə̄'rtin*)	
morn	*mǭ'rn*	morning
orchard	*ǭ'tšə'rt*	orchard
ort	*ǭ'rts*	broken victuals.

b) = *ə̄r*.

coral	*kərəl*	coral
corn	*kə̄'rn*	corn
cnorre	*knə̄'r*	knot in a tree
for	*fə̄'r*	for
fortune	*fə̄'tin*	fortune
	(*fǭ'rtin*)	
horn	*hə̄'rn*	horn
mord	*mə'rþ*	a great quantity
þorn	*þə̄'rn*	thorn.

2. ME. *o* + *ŋ* = *uŋ*.

among	*əmuŋg*	among
along	*əluŋg*	along
belongen	*biluŋg*	belong
dongen	*duŋg*	struck (ppl.)

ME.	OD.	NE.
(lang) long	*luŋg*	long
(sang) song	*suŋg*	song
(strang) strong	*struŋg*	strong
(tange) tonge	*tuŋg*	tongs
(throng) thrung	*þruŋg*	throng
(wrang) wrong	*ruŋg* (*roŋg*) (*roŋk*)	wrong.

Note: *roŋk* is an Ashton importation, cp. Indroduction.

3. a) Before *l*, *s*, *t*, ME. *ol* = *au*.

ME.	OD.	NE.
bolle	*bau*	bowl (sb.)
bolster	*baustǝʳ*	bolster
bolt	*baut*	bolt
colt	*kaut*	colt
pollen	*pau*	to cut
tol	*tau*	toll.

b) Before *k* ME. *ol* = *ǫ*.

folk	*fǫk (fok)*	folk
ʒolk	*jǫk*	yolk.

u.

1. Spontaneous Development.

A. English Sources.

§ 11.

ME. *u* appears in the OD. as *u* and *ụ*. It is often difficult to decide which is the correct form, the latter predominating before *m*, *n*, *ŋ*.

1. ME. *u* = OE. *u*.

ME.	OD.	NE.
bull	*bul (bīf)*	tough beef
bunden	*bund*	bound
butere	*butǝʳ* *butđǝʳ*	butter
cumen	*kụmn*	come (p. pl.)
cuppe-bōrd	*kubǝʳt*	cup-board
drunken	*druŋkn* *đruŋkn*	drunk
dubben	*dub*	to clip anything with a smooth edge

ME.	OD.	NE.
dun + ock	*dụnǝk*	a hedge-sparrow
grund	*grụn(d)*	ground
hund(red)	*unǝʳt* *ụndǝʳt* *ụndđǝʳt*	hundred
Lunden	*Lụnǝn*	London
luven	*luv*	to love
pund	*pụnd*	pound
scruf	*skrụf*	scurf
sumhwat	*sụmǝt*	something
sumbodiʒ	*sụmbri*	somebody
tunne	*tụn*	to pour liquor into casks
þuner	*þunǝʳ*	thunder
þurh	*þruf* (*þrū*)	through
wunien	*wụn*	live
wunder	*wụnđǝʳ*	wonder.

ME.	OD.	NE.		ME.	OD.	NE.
	2. ME. u = OE. y.			schutte	šut	shut
bundel	bundil	bundle		trundel	trundl	trundle
crucche	krutš	crutch				

B. Scandinavian Sources.

luggen	lug	to pull		ruke	ruk	a large
muck	muk	filth				quantity
puffen	pufl	to breathe with difficulty				

C. ME. u from other Teutonic Sources.

plumpen	plump	straight to the point		slutte	slut	a slover woman
frumplen	frumpt	vexed				

D. French Sources.

busard	buzərt	a large moth		gumme (gomme)	gum	gum
bulge	bulš	to bulge		musel (mosel)	muz	mouth
cruste	krusəz krusiz	crusts		stubl	stubl	stubble
flux	fluks	excited state of mind		summe (somme)	sum	sum.

E. Celtic Sources.

ME.	OD.	NE.
crudde	krud	curds.

F. Unknown Sources.

ME.	OD.	NE.		ME.	OD.	NE.
chuffe	tšuf	surly		sluche	slutš	half m
crumpe	krump	cramp				snow.
hukken	ukl	to stoop		Note: ME. u (o) also app
mum	mum	quiet		as o in the following cases,
punchen	puns	to kick		bably thus: $u > u > o$?
ruckelen	rukl	to rattle		cumen		
scunneren	skunər	to dislike		comen	kom (kum) come
schunten	šunt	to move on				

ME.	OD.	NE.
comforten	*komfǝ*ʳ*t* (*kumfǝ*ʳ*t*)	comfort
dromme	*drom* (*drum*)	drum
knokel	*nokelz* [1]	knuckles
sum (som)	*som* (*sum*) some	some
sumbodiʒ	*sombri* *somdi* *sumbri* *sumdi*	somebody

ME.	OD.	NE.
stump, stomp	*stomp* (*stump*)	stump
trumpet	*trompit* (*trumpit*) (*þrumpit*)	trumpet
up	*op* (*up*)	up.

2. Development in Combination.

§ 12.

1. ME. $u + r = ŏ̆^r$.

burlen	*bŏ̆rl*	to pour
burre	*bŏ̆r*	a sticky plant
hurren	(*h*)*ŏ̆r*	to purr
hurst	*hŏ̆rst*	a wood, grove
murđren	*mŏ̆rđǝr*	murder
murnen	*mŏ̆rn*	mourn
wurchen	*wŏ̆rtš*	to work
wurʒen	*wǝrit*	to worry.

2. ME. $u + l$ (final) or before $l, d, t = ū$ or $ū + đ$ or t.

bulder (stōn)	*būđǝr*	boulder
culter ful	*kūđǝr* *fū*	ploughshare full
pullen	*pū*	pull
schulder	*šūđǝr* (*šūdǝr*) (*šilđǝr*)	shoulder.

ü.

A. English Sources.

§ 13.

ME. *ü* = OE. *y* has become ME. *i* in NW. Midland-Dialect = OD. *i* (cf. § 7, A, b.), but in the following OE. *y* > OD. *u.*

ME.	OD.	NE.	ME.	OD.	NE.
bündel	*bundl*	bundle	schütel	*šutl*	shuttle
schütten	*šut*	shut	þrüssche	*þruš*	thrush.

---

[1] No other form.

B. French Sources.

ME. *u* = Fr. *ü* = OD. *u* (*u̞*).

ME.	OD.	NE.
duchesse	*dutšəs*	duchess
humble	*u̞mbl*	humble
juǧe	*dǯu̞dǯ*	judge

Note: Cp. § 7 and 8.

ME.	OD.	NE.
just	*dǯust*	just
justice	*dǯustis*	justice
punisshe	*pu̞nis*	punish
studie	*studi*	study.

Long Vowels.

ā.

1 Spontaneous Development.

A. English Sources.

§ 14.

ME. *ā* appears as *ē*, when final or before voiced consonants, as *ēⁱ* before unvoiced.

a) ME. *ā* = OE. *a.*

1. = OD. *ē.*

ME.	OD.	NE.
āken	*ēk*	ache
drāke	*drēk*	drake
hāte	*(h)ēt*	hate
lāke	*lēk*	lake
nāked	*nēkt*	naked
snāke	*snēk*	snake
stāpel	*stēpl*	staple
ᵗāper	*tēpəʳ*	taper.

2. = OD. *ēⁱ.*

grāse	*grēⁱz*	graze
grāve	*grēⁱv*	grave
knāve	*neⁱv*	knave

ME.	OD.	NE.
lāde	*lēⁱd*	lade
wāde	*wēⁱd*	wade
māne	*mēⁱn*	mane
māme	*nēⁱm*	name
sāme	*seⁱm*	same
spāde	*spēⁱd*	spade
tāle	*tēⁱl*	tale.

b) ME. *ā* = OE. *ea.*

āle	*ēⁱl*	ale
gāte	*gēt*	gete
schāde	*sēⁱd*	shade.

c) ME. *ā* = OE. *æ.*

blād	*blēⁱd*	blade
māpel	*mēpl*	maple
rāven	*rēⁱvn*	raven
wāter	*wētəʳ*	water.
	(wētđəʳ)	
	(watəʳ)	

B. Scandinavian Sources.

gāpe	*gēp*	gape	gāse	*gēⁱz*	gaze
gāte	*gēt*	way, road	cāke	*kēk*	cake.

C. French Sources.

ME.	OD.	NE.	ME.	OD.	NE.
āble	$\bar{e}^ibl$	able	fāble	$f\bar{e}^ibl$	fable
bācon	$b\bar{e}kn$	bacon	fāce	$f\bar{e}s$	face
bācin	$b\bar{e}sn$	basin	fame	$f\bar{e}^im$	fame
blāme	$bl\bar{e}^im$	blame	māsoun	$m\bar{e}sn$	mason
caǧe	$k\breve{e}^id\breve{z}$	cage	nāture	$n\bar{e}t\partial^r$	nature
cās	$k\bar{e}s$	case		$(n\bar{e}t\partial^r)$	
debāte	$dib\bar{e}t$	debate	plācc	$pl\bar{e}s$	place.
escāpen	$esk\bar{e}p$	escape			

2. Development in Combination.

§ 15.

ME. $\bar{a} + r$ = OD. $\bar{\partial}^r$ (very long).

			spārcn	$sp\bar{\partial}^r$	spare
			stāre	$st\bar{\partial}^r$	stare.
fāre	$f\bar{\partial}^r$	fare			
hāre	$h\bar{\partial}^r$	hare			
kāreles	$k\bar{\partial}^rl\partial s$	careless			

Note: For a shortening of ME. $\bar{a}$ to $\breve{a}$ see special chapter on long Vowels shortened in OD.

$\bar{e}$.

I. $\bar{e}$.

1. Spontaneous Development.

A. English Sources.

§ 16.

1. ME. $\bar{e}$ = OE. $\bar{e}a$.

a) = OD. $\bar{\imath}\partial$, je.

OE.	ME.	OD.	NE.
bẹ̄am	bẹ̄m	$b\bar{\imath}\partial m$	beam
bẹ̄an	bẹ̄ne	$b\bar{\imath}\partial n$	bean
bẹ̄atan	bẹ̄te	$b\bar{\imath}\partial t, bjet$	beat
brẹ̄ad	brẹ̄d	$br\bar{\imath}\partial d$	bread
čẹ̄ap	chẹ̄p	$t\check{s}\bar{\imath}\partial p (t\check{s}\breve{e}p)$	cheap
dẹ̄ad	dẹ̄d	$d\bar{\imath}\partial d, djed$	dead
dẹ̄af	dẹ̄f	$d\bar{\imath}\partial f$	deaf
dẹ̄aþ	dẹ̄þ	$d\bar{\imath}\partial þ, dje þ$	death
drẹ̄am	drẹ̄m	$dr\bar{\imath}\partial m (dr\breve{e}m)$	dream

OE.	ME.	OD.	NE.
hẹafod	hēd	*jed*	head
hẹap	hēp	*īəp*	heap
lẹaf	lēf	*līəf*	leaf
hlẹapan	lēpe	*lǣp*	leap
sẹam	sēm	*sīəm*	seam
stẹam	stēm	*stīəm*	steam
strẹam	strēm	*strīəm*	stream.

b) = OD. *ī*, probably influenced by the lit. language.

| ẹast | ēst | *īst* | east |
| stẹap | stēp | *stīp* | steep. |

c) = OD. *ę̄*.

| ẹastro | ēster | *ę̄stəʳ, ēsþəʳ* | Easter |
| grẹat | grēt | *ġrę̄t* | great. |

2. ME. *ę̄* = OE. *ǣ* (Germ. *ai + i, j*).

a) = OD. *īə, je*.

clǣnc	clę̄ne	*tlīen (tlen)*	clean
dǣl	dę̄l	*dīəl, djel*	deal
hǣlan	hę̄le	*īəl, jel*	heal
hǣte	hę̄te	*īət, jet*	heat
hǣþ	hę̄þ	*īeþ, jeþ*	heath
lǣdan	lę̄de	*līəd, ljed*	lead
hlǣnc	lę̄ne	*līən*	lean
lǣst	lę̄st	*līəst*	least
lǣfan	lę̄ve	*līəv*	leave
ʒemǣne	mę̄ne	*mīən*	mean (adj)
mǣnan	mę̄ne	*mīən*	mean (vb.)
rǣccan	rę̄che	*rīəts (rēts)*	reach
sprǣdan	sprę̄de	*sprīed*	spread
swǣtan	swę̄te	*swīət (swot)*	sweat
hwǣte	whę̄te	*wīət*	wheat.

b) = OD. *ę̄*.

| sǣ | sę̄ | *sę̄ (sī)* | sea |
| tǣčian | tę̄che | *tę̄ts* | teach. |

c) = OD. *ī*.

| sǣ | sę̄ | *sī (sę̄)* | sea. |

d) = OD. *ŏ*.

| swǣtan | swę̄te | *swot (swīət)* | sweat. |

B. French Sources.

The vast majority of genuine dialect words from the French show a development of ME. $\bar{e}$ to $\bar{e}$.

I. ME. $\bar{e}$ = Fr. *ai, ei*.

a) = OD. $\bar{e}$ ($\bar{e}^i$).

Fr.	ME.	OD.	NE.
aise	ẹse	$\bar{e}^i z$	ease
aigle	ẹ̄gle	$\bar{e}gl$	eagle
eigre	ẹ̄gre	$\bar{e}gə^r$	eager
pais	pẹ̄s	$p\bar{e}s$	peace
raison	rẹ̄soun	$r\bar{e}zn$ [$rīəzn,$ $rezn, rjezn$]	reason
traitier	trẹ̄ten (traiten)	$tr\bar{e}t$	treat.
graisse	grẹ̄se	$gr\bar{e}s$	grease

b) = OD. $\bar{i}ə$, *je*.

plaisir	plẹ̄se	$pl\bar{i}əz$ (*plez*)	please
raison	rẹ̄soun	$r\bar{i}əzn, rjezn,$ [$r\bar{e}zn, rezn$]	reason
saison	sẹ̄soun	$s\bar{i}əzn$	season
saisir	sẹ̄sen (saisen)	$s\bar{i}ɔz$	seize.

c) = OD. $\bar{i}$ (influenced by the lit. language).

desaise	disẹ̄ze	$diz\bar{i}z$	disease
encreiss-	encrẹ̄sen	$inkr\bar{i}z$	increase
fait	fẹ̄t	$f\bar{i}t$	feat
faiture	fẹ̄ture	$f\bar{i}tšər$	feature
plaidier	plẹ̄de	$pl\bar{i}d$	plead.

II. ME. $\bar{e}$ = Fr. *e*.

a) = OD. $\bar{e}$.

deceveir	decẹve (deceive)	$dis\bar{e}v$	deceive
prechier	prẹ̄chen	$pr\bar{e}tš$	preach
recet	recẹ̄t (receit)	$ris\bar{e}t$	receipt.

b) = OD. $\bar{i}ə$.

beste	bẹste	$b\bar{i}əst$	beast
feste	fẹ̄ste	$f\bar{i}əst$	feast
receveir	recẹve (receive)	$res\bar{i}əv$	receive.

c) = OD. *ī* (literary influence).

Fr.	ME.	OD.	NE.
appeler	apę̄le	əpīl	appeal
cesser	cę̄se	sīs	cease.

III. ME. *ę̄* = Fr. *ëe* = OD. *īə*.

sëel	sę̄le	sīəl	seal
vëel	vę̄l	vīəl	veal.

2. Development in Combination.

§ 17.

ME. *ę̄r* = OD. *īəʳ*.

bę̄ard	bę̄rd	bīəʳd	beard
ę̄are	ę̄re	īəʳ	ear
nę̄ar	nę̄r	nīəʳ	near
tę̄ar	tę̄r	tīəʳ	tear (sb.).

II. *ē̦*.

1. Spontaneous Development.

A. English Sources.

§ 18.

1. ME. *ē̦* = OE. *ē̦* (*ō* + *i, j*).

a) = OD. *ī*.

bēče	bēche	bītš	beech
blēdan	blēde	blīd	bleed
brēč	brēche	brītšəz	breeches
fēdan	fēde	fīd	feed
fēlan	fēle	fīl	feel
fēt	fēt	fīt	feet
gēs	gēs	gīs	geese
grēne	grēne	grīn	green
grētan	grēten	grīt	weep
sēcan	sēke, sēche	sītš	seek
twēte	swēte	swīt	sweet
sēþ	tēth	tīþ	teeth.

b) = OD. *īə, je*.

brēdan	brēde	brīəd	breed
mētan	mēte	mīət, mjet	meet
spēd	spēd	spīəd	speed.

2. ME. ẹ̄ = OE. ẹ̄ = WG. ē final.

a) = OD. ī.

OE.	ME.	OD.	NE.
hẹ̄	hẹ̄	ī (ĭ) (ə̄)	he
mẹ̄	mẹ̄	mī (mĭ)	me
þẹ̄	þẹ̄	dī (dĭ)	thee
wẹ	wẹ̄	wī (wĭ)	we.

b) = OD. ĭ.

hē̦	hẹ̄	ĭ (ī) (ə̄)	he
mē̦	mẹ̄	mĭ [mī]	me
þẹ̄	þẹ̄	dĭ [dī]	thee
wẹ̄	wẹ̄	wĭ [wī]	we.

c) = OD. ə̄.

hẹ̄	hẹ̄	ə̄ (ī) (ĭ)	he.

Note: The forms with ī are stressed, those with ĭ or ə̄ unstressed.

3. ME. ẹ̄ = OE. ẹ̄o.

a) = OD. ī.

bẹ̄on	bẹ̄	bī (bĭ)	be
bẹ̄o	bẹ̄	bī	bee
cẹ̄oke	chẹ̄ke	tšīk	cheek
dẹ̄op	dẹ̄p	dīp	deep
dẹ̄ofol	dẹ̄vel	dīl (divl) (dēl, djūl) }	devil
frẹ̄osan	frẹ̄se	frīz	freeze
lẹ̄of	lẹ̄f	līf (lẹ̄f)	lief
sẹ̄on	sẹ̄	sī	see
þẹ̄of	thẹ̄f	þīf	thief
wẹ̄od	wẹ̄d	wīd	weed
hwẹ̄ol	whẹ̄l	wīl	wheel.

b) = OD. īə.

crẹ̄opan	crẹ̄pe	krīep	creep

c) = OD. ẹ̄.

dẹ̄ofol	dẹ̄vel	dēl (dīl, divl, djūl)	devil
lẹ̄of	lẹ̄f	lẹ̄f (līf)	lief.

- 32 -

d) = OD. *ĭ*.

OE.	ME.	OD.	NE.
bēon	bēn	*bin (bīn)*	been
bēon	bē̜	*bi (bī)*	be
dēofol	dēvel	*divl*	devil
sēoc	sēk	*sik*	sick.

e) = OD. *jū*.

dēofol	dēvel	*djūl*	devil.

4. ME. ē̜ = OE. ē̜ (ē̜a + i, j)

a) = OD. *ī*.

ʒelēfan	bilēve	*bilīv*	believe
sċēte	schēte	*šīt*	sheet
stē̜pel	stē̜pel	*stīpə*	steeple
tēʒan	tē̜ge (tīge)	*tī*	tie.

b) = OD. *īə*.

nēd	nē̜d (ṇē̜d)	*nīəd*	need
slēfe	slē̜ve	*slīəv*	sleeve.

5. ME. ē̜ = OE. ē̜ + ld.

a) = OD. *ī*.

fēld	fē̜ld	*fīlt (fēlt)*	field
ʒēldan	ʒē̜lde	*jīld*	yield.

b) = OD. *ē̜*.

fē̜ld	fē̜ld	*fē̜lt (fīlt)*	field.

B. French Sources.

ME. ē̜ = OD. *ī*:

1. ME. ē = Fr. é = OD. *ī*.

agréer	agrēe	*əgrī*	agree
légende	lēgende	*līdžənd*	legend.

2. ME. ē̜ = Fr. ie = OD. *ī*.

chief	chēf	*tšīf*	chief
niece	nē̜ce	*nīs*	niece
piece	pē̜ce	*pīs*	peace.

3. ME. ē̜ + a = Fr. ea = OD. *ié*.

theatre	tē̜atre	*þiétə^r*	theatre.

4. ME. ę̄ = Fr. ué = OD. ī̯ə.

OFr.	ME.	OD.	NE.
buéf	bȩ̄f	*bī̯əf*	beef
puéple	pȩ̄ple	*pī̯əpl*	people.

5. ME. ę̄ = Fr. *e, ié.*

a) = OD. ī.

degre	degrȩ̄	*digrī*	degree
relever	relȩ̄ve	*rilīv*	relieve
succeder	succȩ̄de	*suksīd*	succeed.

b) = OD. ī̯ə.

grié f, grēf	grēf	*grī̯əf*	grief
grever	grȩ̄ve	*grī̯əv*	grieve.

c) = OD. ȩ̄.

(L) febrem	fȩ̄ver	*fȩ̄və^r*	fever
obedient	obȩ̄dient	*obēdjənt*	obedient
special	spȩ̄cial	*spȩ̄šəl*	special.

§ 19.

1. ME. ę̄ before *r* in English Words.

a) ME. ę̄r = OE. ę̄r (*ō* + *i, j*).

a) = OD. ī̯ə^r.

wēriʒ	wȩ̄ry	*wī̯əri (wēəri)**	weary.

b) = OD. ēə^r.

wēriʒ	wȩ̄ry	*wēəri (wī̯əri)*	weary.

b) ME. ę̄r = OE. ēr = WG. ē (final).

hȩ̄r	hȩ̄re	*ī̯ə^r*	here.

c) ME. ę̄r = OE. ę̄or = OD. ī̯ə^r.

bȩ̄or	bȩ̄r	*bī̯ə^r*	bear
dȩ̄ore	dȩ̄re	*dī̯ə^r*	dear
dȩ̄or	dȩ̄r	*dī̯ə^r*	deer
drȩ̄oriʒ	drȩ̄ri	*drī̯əri*	dreary.

* Note: The form *drī* is more common in the OD.

2. ME. ę̄ before *r* in French Words.

1. ME. ȩ̄r = Fr. *ier.*

a) = OD. ī̯ə^r.

fiers	fȩ̄rs	*fī̯ə^rs*	fierce
piere	pȩ̄re	*pī̯ə^r*	pier.

3

2. ME. *ẹ̈r* = *aier* = OD. *aiə͏ʳ*.

OFr.	ME.	OD.	NE.
quaier	quẹ̈r (quaer)	*kwaiə͏ʳ*	quire.

3. ME. *ẹ̈r* = Fr. *œur* = OD. *aiə͏ʳ*.

chœur	quẹ̈r	*kwaiə͏ʳ*	choir.

4. ME. *ẹ̈r* = Fr. *er*.

a) = OD. *īə͏ʳ*.

aperer	apẹ̈re	*əpīə͏ʳ*	appear
cler	clẹ̈r	*ltīə͏ʳ*	clear
fers (fiers)	fẹ̈rs	*fīə͏ʳs*	fierce.
chere	chẹ̈re	*tšīə͏ʳ*	cheer.

b) = OD. *aiə͏ʳ*.

enquer-	enquẹ̈re	*inkwaieʳ*	enquire.
frere	frẹ̈re	*fraiə͏ʳ*	friar.

III. ME. *ẹ̈* – *ę̄* from. W. Germ. *ā*.

1. Spontaneous Development.

A. English Sources.

§ 20.

1. ME. *ẹ̄* — *ę̄* = OE. *ę̄, ǣ*.

a) = OD. *īə*.

brǣđ	brēth	*brīəþ*	breath
brǣþan	brēþen	*brīəđ*	breathe
on-drǣdan	drēd	*drīəd*	dread
nǣdl	nēdle	*nīədl* (*nīld, nīl*) }	needle
scǣp	schēp	*šīəp*	sheep
slǣpan	slēpe	*slīəp*	sleep
stǣle	stēle	*stīəl*	steel
strǣt	strēte	*strīət*	street
þrǣd	thrēd	*þrīəd*	thread.

b) = OD. *ī*.

OE.	ME.	OD.	NE.
dǣd	dēd	*dīd*	deed
ǣl	ēl	*īl*	eel
ǣfnung	ēvoning	*īn*	evening
grǣdiȝ	grēdi	*grīdi*	greedy
nǣdl	nēdle	*nīld, nīl* *(nīədl)* }	needle
sǣd	sēd	*sīd*	seed.

c) = OD. *ę̄*.

spǣč	spēcho	*spę̄tš*	speech.

d) = OD. *ūə*.

hǣr	hēr	*jūəʳ*	hair.

e) = OD. *ī*.

in + stǣde	instēde	*istid*	instead
rǣdels	rēdles	*ridl*	riddle.

2. Development in Combination.

§ 21.

ME. *ę̄* – *ę̄* + *r* = OE. *ēr, ǣr*.

1. = OD. *iəʳ*.

bǣr	bēre	*bīəʳ*	bier
fǣr	fēre	*fīəʳ*	fear.

2. = OD. *əʳ*.

wǣron	wēre	*wəʳ*	were
hwǣr	wēhr	*wəʳ (wīəʳ)*	where.

IV. Medium *ē* = OE. *ë* in Open Syllables.

(cp. Luick, Untersuchungen § 202.)

1. Spontaneous Development.

§ 22.

a) = OD. *iə, jə*.

cnëdan	knę̄de	*nīəd (ned)*	knead
mëlo	mę̄l	*mīəl, mjel* *(mę̄l)* }	meal
stëlan	stę̄le	*stīəl, stjel* *(stę̄l)* }	steal
trëdan	trę̄de	*trīəd (trę̄d)*	tread.

3*

b) = OD. ę̄.

OE.	ME.	OD.	NE.
brĕcan	brę̄ke	*brę̄k*	break
ĕtan	ę̄tē	*ę̄t*	eat
mĕlo	mę̄l	*mę̄l* (*mīəl, mjel*) }	meal
spĕcan	spę̄ke	*spę̄k*	speak
stĕlan	stę̄le	*stę̄l* (*stīəl, stjel*) }	steal
trēdan	trę̄de	*trę̄d (trīed)*	tread
wĕfan	wę̄ve	*wę̄v*	weave.

c) = OD *ī*.

brĕcan + fæstan	brę̄kefaste	*brīkfəst*	breakfast.

2. Development in Combination.

§ 23.

1. ME. ę̄r = OE. ĕ- before *r*.

a) = OD. *īər*.

scĕran	schę̄re	*šīər*	shear
spĕre	spę̄re	*spīər*	spear.

b) = OD. *ę̄ər*.

bĕra	bę̄re	*bę̄ər*	bear (sb.)
bĕran	bę̄re	*bę̄ər (bər)*	bear (vb.)
pĕru	pę̄re	*pę̄ər (pə̄r)*	pear
tĕran	tę̄re	*tę̄ər (tə̄r)*	tear (vb.).

c) = OD. *ə̄r*.

bĕran	bę̄re	*bə̄r (bə̄ər)*	bear (vb.)
pĕru	pę̄re	*pə̄r (pə̄ər)*	pear
tĕran	tę̄re	*tə̄r (tə̄ər)*	tear (vb.).

2. ME. ę̄r = OE. e- before *r*.

a) = OD. *ē̄ər*.

swĕrian	swę̄re	*swę̄ər (swə̄r)*	swear
wĕrian	wę̄re	*wē̄ər*	wear.

b) = OD. *ə̄r*.

swĕrian	swę̄re	*swə̄r (swē̄ər)*	swear.

V.

§ 24.

In the following words *ē* (from various sources) has had *j* prefixed.

OE.	ME.	OD.	NE.
āl	ę̄l	*jel*	awl
ǣrlice	ę̄rli	*jarli*	early
ę̄are	ę̄re	*jïəˊ*	ear
eornust	ę̄rnest	*jǭrnest,järnest*	earnest
eorđe	ę̄rthe	*jəˊþ*	earth
Fr. aise	ę̄se + y	*jezi*	easy
ĕtan	ę̄te	*jet*	eat.

Ī.

1. Spontaneous Development.

A. English Sources.

§ 25.

ME. *ī* has two developments in the OD. becoming either *əi*, the older form or *ai* as in the literary language.

1. a) ME.*ī* = OE. *ī* = OD. *əi*.

ME.	OD.	NE.
finde	*fəind*	find
five	*fəiv*	five
hwīle	*wəil (wol)*	while
mīle	*məil*	mile
mīn	*məin*	mine
pīpe	*pəip*	pipe
rīden	*rəid*	ride
sīde	*səid*	side
schīnen	*šəin*	shine
strīken	*strəik*	strike
tīme	*təim*	time
wīf	*wəif*	wife
wīlde	*wəild*	wild

ME.	OD.	NE.
wīnden	*wəint*	wind
wrīten	*rəit*	write.

b) Forms where *ai* is preferred, though *əi* is also found. In some cases the words are not in common use in the dialect.

chīmbe	*tšaim (tsəim)*	chime
climben	*tlaim (tləim)*	climb
grīnden	*graind (grəind)*	grind
līf	*laif (ləif)*	life
mīlde	*maild (məild)*	mild
sīde	*saiđ*	scythe
swīn	*swain*	swine.

c) Forms where I have only heard *ai*. They are either foreign to the dialect or strongly influenced by the lit. language.

ME.	OD.	NE.
abīden	əbaid	bear, put up with
arīsen	əraiz	arise
bɪnden	baind	bind
Chrīst	kraist	Christ
īs	ais	ice
īdel	aidl[1]	idle
īlond	ailənd	island
līne	lain	line
whīt	wait	white
wīd	waid	wide
wīn	wain	wine
wīse	waiz	wise.

2. ME. ī = OE. *y*.

a) = OD. *əi*.

ME.	OD.	NE.
bīle	bəil	boil (tumour)
dīven	dəiv	dive
hīde	həid	hide (skin)
hīden	həid	to hide
hīve	əiv	hive
līs	ləis	lice
mīs	məis	mice
minde	məind	mind
tīnen	təin (tīn)	to shut.

ME.	OD.	NE.

b) = OD. *ai*.

ME.	OD.	NE.
bīle	bail	bile
brīde	braid	bride
kīnde	kaind	kind
prīde	praid	pride.

c) = OD. *ɪ*.

ME.	OD.	NE.
tīnen	tīn (təin)	shut
wīschen	wīš	wish.

d) = OD. *ɪ̆*.

ME.	OD.	NE.
lītel	litl	little
thīmel	þimbl	thimble.

3. ME. ī = OE. *i (ē), y -* = OD. *əi* or *ai*.

ME.	OD.	NE.
bīe (bɪğğe)	bəi	buy
drīze	drəi	dry
nīne	nəin	nine
rīe	rai	rye
stīle	stail (stəil)	stile
tīe	təi	tie
tīle	tail	tile
tīthe	taið	tithe.

4. ME. ī = OE. *ēo + ?*

| flīe | flāi (fləi) | fly |
| līe | lāi | to tell l |

5. ME. ī = OE. *ēa + ?*

| (eie), ɪe | əi | eye. |

B. French Sources.

a) ME. ī = OD. *əi*.

fīne	fəin	fine
nīce	nəis	nice
quīete	kwəiət	quiet

sīgne	səin	sign
spīt	spəit	spite
strīf	strəif	strife
strīve	strəiv	strive.

---

[1] A most uncommon word in OD. It is always expressed by *lēzi* = l

b) = OD. *ai* or *əi*.

ME.	OD.	NE.
fīnal	*fainəl* (*fəinəl*) }	final
līoun	*laiən* (*ləiən*	lion
pīnte	*paint* (*pəint*) }	pint
sīlent	*suilənt* (*səilent*)[1] }	silent.

c) ME. *ī* = OD. *ai*.

avīs	*ədvāis*	advice
apetīt	*apətāit*	appetite

ME.	OD.	NE.
Bīble	*Baibl*	Bible
crīe	*krāi*	cry
delīte	*dilāit*	delight
denīe	*dināi*	deny
dīamaund	*dāimənt*	diamond
gīaunt	*dzāient*	giant
lībrairie	*lāibrəri*	library
prīs	*prāis*	price
(prīvē)	*prāivət*	private
resīgnen	*rizāin*	resign
tīgre	*tāigər*	tiger
vīce	*vāis*	vice
vīolent	*vāilent*	violent.

C. Scandinavian Sources.

ME. *ī* = OD. *ai, əi*.

dīe	*dəi*	die

skīe	*skai* *skəi* }	sky
thrīve	*þraiv*	thrive.

ME. *ī* in Combination.

§ 26.

ME. *ī* + *r* gives the triphthongs *āiər* and *əiər* in the OD.

desīre	*dizāiər*	desire
empīre	*Empəiər*	Empire
fīr	*fəiər*	fire
hīren	*həiər*	hire
īren	*əiərn*	iron
mīre	*məiər*	mire
schīre	*šāiər*	shire

squīre	*skwaiər*	squire
wīr	*wəiər*	wire.

Note: "Empire" being a common name for music halls and theatres it has become an integral part of the Dialect an has conformed to the usual Sound Law.

---

[1] *səilent* is rare, *kwəiət* is the more commonly used word.

$\bar{Q}$.

1. Spontaneous Development.

A. English Sources.

§ 27.

I. ME. $\bar{q}$ becomes $\bar{u}\partial$ in the OD.

1. ME. $\bar{q}$ = OE. $\bar{a}$.

ME.	OD.	NE.
alǭne	əlū̄ən	alono
bǭt	bū̄ət	boat
bǭn	bū̄ən	bone
bǭthe	bū̄əþ	both
	(bwoþ)	
clǭth	tlū̄əz	clothes
gǭ	gū̄ə (gū)	go
grǭne	grū̄ən	groan
hǭm	ū̄əm (wom)	home
lǭf	lū̄əf	loaf
mǭst	mū̄əst	most
	(mwost)	
nǭse	nū̄əz	nose
ǭtes	ū̄əts (wots)	oats
ǭþ	uəþ	oath
rǭde	rū̄əd (rǭd)	road
sǭpe	sū̄əp	soap
	(swop)	
stǭn	stū̄ən	stone
þǭs	dū̄əz (dū̄z)	those.

2. ME. $\bar{q}$ = OE. o.

cǭle	kū̄əl (koil)	coal
flǭte	flū̄ət	float
rǭse	rū̄əz	rose
smǭke	smū̄ək	smoke(sb.)*
þrǭte	þrū̄ət	throat.

* Note: The dialect word for "smoke" as a verb is rī̄tš.

II. In a number of wo ME. $\bar{q}$ has become $\bar{o}$.

ME.	OD.	NE.
arǭs	ərǭz	arose
at-ǭn	ətǭn	atone
bǭste	bǭst	boast
brǭche	brǭtš	broach
gǭte	gǭt	goat
grǭte	grǭt	groat
hǭp	hǭp	hope
mǭne	mǭn	moan
ǭc	ǭk	oak
sǭ (swo)	sǭ	so
tǭ	tǭ	toe.

Note: These cases where I $\bar{q}$ = $\bar{o}$ are probably due eithe the influence of lit. English or that of the adjoining west dialects. Cp. Hargreaves § 4

III. ME. $\bar{q}$ = wo, wu.

bǭn	bwon	bone
	(bū̄ən)	
bǭthe	bwoþ	both
	(bū̄əþ)	
cǭt	kwot	coat
	(kū̄ət)	
gǭ	gwo	go
	(gū̄ə)	
hǭl	wol (wul)	whole
hǭm	wom	home
	(wum)	

ME.	OD.	NE.
hǭt	wot	hot
lǭde	lwod	load
	(lūəd)	
mǭst	mwoost	most
	(mūəst)	
ǭn	won	one*
	(wṳn)	
ǭnes	wonst	once
	(wṳnst)	
ǭtes	wots	oats
	(wṳts)	
sǭpe	swop	soap
	(sūəp)	
tǭde	twod	toad.
	(tūəd)	

* Note: "The one" is however t'ǭn.

IV. There still remain a number of forms with peculiar developments.

ME.	OD.	NE.
cǭle	koil(kūəl)	coal
hǭle	oil	hole
gǭ	gū (gūə)	go
gǭn	gṳn	gone
shǭn	šun	shone
sǭry	sūri	sorry
þǭs	ðūz (ðūəz)	those.

Note: The forms "koil" and "oil" are probably importations from the neighbouring West Riding of Yorkshire. Cp. Wright § 109.

B. French Sources.

ME.	OD.	NE.	ME.	OD.	NE.
clǭse	tlūəs (tlūs)	close	rǭste	rūəst	roast
cǭt	kūət	coat	tǭste	tūəst	toast.
	(kwot)				

2. Development in Combination.

§ 28.

1. ME. ǭ + l before d = au in OD.

ME.	OD.	NE.
ɔehǭlde	bihaud	behold
ɔǭld	baud	bold
fǭld	faut	fold
ʒǭld	gaud	gold
	(gūld)[1]	
ʒǭlden	gaudn	golden
	(gūldn)	
ɪǭlde	haud	hold
;ld	aud	old

sǭld	saud	sold
tǭld	taud	told.

2. ME. ǭ + r mostly follows the general rule becoming ūər.

bifǭren	bifūər	before
	(bifǭr)	
glǭrie	dlūəri	glory
hǭrse	ūərs	hoarse
mǭre	mūər	more
rǭre	rūə	roar
sǭr	sūər	sore.

---

[1] From ME. gōld.

But ME. ǭ is retained in:

ME.	OD.	NE.
bǭren	bǭ͡rn	born
bifǭren	bifǭ͡r	before
	(bifūə͡r)	

ME.	OD.	NE.
lǭrd	lǭrd	lord
ǭver	ǭə͡r (ūə͡r)	over
swǭren	swǭ͡rn	sworn.

ō̧.

1. Spontaneous Development.

A. English Sources.

§ 29.

ME. ǭ becomes ū̧ in the OD. as in the lit. language.

1. a) ME. ǭ = OE. ǭ.

ME.	OD.	NE.
brǭm	brū̧m	broom
cǭl	kū̧l	cool
dǭm	dū̧m	doom
dǫn	dū̧	do
fǫde	fū̧d	food
glǭm	glū̧m	gloom
gǭme	gū̧ms	gums
gǭs	gū̧s	goose
hǫf	hū̧f	hoof
mǭd	mū̧d	mood
mǭder	mū̧dər	mother
	(mū̧dər)	
mǫne	mū̧n	moon
	(mūən)	
nǫn	nū̧n	noon
pǭl	pū̧	pool
prǫve	prū̧v	prove
rǫde	rū̧d	rood
rǫf	rū̧f	roof
rǫte	rū̧t	root
scǭle	skū̧	school
schǫ	šū̧	shoe
smǫthe	smū̧t	smooth
sǫne	sū̧n	soon

ME.	OD.	NE.
stǫl	stū̧	stool
tǫ	tū̧	too
tǫl	tū̧l	tool.

Note: The form gū may also originate in an old ME. gǭ, cf. Luick §§ 143, 144.

b) ME. ǭ = OE. a.

whǫ	hū̧	who
hwǭm	hū̧m	whom
wǫmbe	wū̧m	womb.

Note: This change of OE. a to ME. ǭ is due to the influence of the preceding w.

2. In a few Words ME. ǭ = OD. ūə.

hūǫs	(h)ūəz	whose
mone	mūən	moon
	(mūn)	
spǭn	spūən	spoon
tōth	tūəp	tooth.

Note: This may be sound-substitution for the Yorkshire ui in these words, cp. Wright § 163.

3. In the following words ere is fluctuation between *ŭ* and for ME. *ọ̄.*

ME.	OD.	NE.
cọ̄k	kŭk	cook
họ̄c	hŭk	hook
lọ̄ke	lŭk	look
mọ̄der	mắdə^r	mother
sọ̄t	sŭt	soot
tọ̄ke	tŭk	took.

ME.	OD.	NE.
ōk	bŭk	book
rọ̄k	brŭk	brook

B. French Sources.

ME. *ọ̄* = French. *o.*

			fọ̄l	fū̆	fool
prọ̄ve	əprūv	approve	mọ̄ve	mūv	move.

2. Development in Combination.

§ 30.

ME. *ọ̄ + r = ū̆ə^r.*

			mọ̄r	mū̆ə^r	moor
ọ̄r	flū̆ə^r	floor	pọ̄vre	pū̆ə^r	poor.
ọ̄r- (duru)[1]	dū̆ə^r (də^r)	door			

ū.

1. Spontaneous Development.

A. English Sources.

§ 31.

ME. *ū* = *eu* in the OD.

1. ME. *ū* = OE. *ū.*

ME.	OD.	NE.
doun	dęun	down
ûwe	bęu	bow (vb)
row	bręu	brow
rown	bręun	brown
loude	klęud	cloud
lout	klęut	rag, blow
ū	kęu	cow
rought	dręut	drought
oul	fęu	foul
round	gręund (grŭn)	ground

ME.	OD.	NE.
hound	hęunt	hound
hous	hęus	house
how	hęu	how
loud	lęud	loud
lous	lęus	louse
mous	męus	mouse
now	nęu	now
out	ęut	out
oule	ęul	owl
pound	pęund (pun(ä))	pound
schroud	šręud	shroud
south	sęuþ	south

---

[1] Cp. Luick, Untersuchungen, § 383 ff.

ME.	OD.	NE.
thou	đẹu (stressed) / đạ (unstr)	thou
thousand	þẹusənt	thousand
toun	tẹun	town
withouten	wiđẹut	without.

2. ME. $\bar{u}$ = OE. $\bar{o}$ before h

ME.	OD.	NE.
bough	bẹu	bough
plough	plẹu	plough.

3. ME. $\bar{u}$ = OE $\breve{u}$ + ʒ.

foul	fẹul	fowl
suʒe	sẹu	sow.

B. French Sources.

1. ME. $\bar{u}$ = AFr. u (o) before nasal.

amounte	əmẹunt	amount
bounde	bẹundəri	boundary
count	kẹunt	count
counte	kẹunti	county
crūne	krẹun (krūn)	crown
fount	fẹuntin	fountain
goun	gẹun	gown
mountaine	mẹuntin	mountain
ounce	ẹuns	ounce
round	rẹund	round.

Note: The form *krūn* = crowi is derived direct from the Lati *corona*.

2. ME. $\bar{u}$ = Fr. ou.

aloue	əlẹu	allow
couche	kẹutš	couch
doute	dẹut	doubt
poudre	pẹuder / peuđər }	powder
route	rẹut	rout.

C. Scandinavian Sources.

Sc. $\bar{u}$ = ME. $\bar{u}$ = OD. ẹu and ẹuə before r.

boun	bẹun	bound
drūpen	drẹup	droop
coure	kẹuər	cower, sit down.

2. Development in Combination.

§ 32.

ME. $\bar{u}$ + r gives a triphthong ẹuər.

bour	bẹuər	bower
couard	keuərd	coward
coure	kẹuər	sit down
devoureu	divẹuər	devour
flour	flẹuər (flȭr)	flower
fiour	flẹuər	flour
houre	ẹuər	hour
pouér	pẹuər	power
schour	šẹuər	shower
tour	tẹuər	tower.

Note 1. Observe however:

flour	flȭr (flẹuər) flower.

Note 2. In cases where liter-
·y English has *ū*, the OD. has
so *ęū* (before labial consonants).

ME.	OD.	NE.
:ūpen	*dręup*	droop
·um	*ręum*	room
oupe	*stęup*	stoop

ME.	OD.	NE.
toumbe	*tęum* (*tōm*) }	tomb
wounde	*węund*	wound (sb).

Cp. Luick, Anglia 16, 501, and
for *wound* cp. Horn, Unters.,
p. 34.

$\bar{\bar{u}}.$

1. Spontaneous Development.

A. English Sources.

§ 33.

ME. *ū* < OE. *ȳ* always became *ī* (cp. § 25, 2) during the ME.
eriod (cf. also *ü* > *i* § 7 b) but:

B. French Sources.

ME. *ū* = French *u* and *ui*
as been mostly retained as *jū*
r *ū* in the OD.

I. ME. *ū* = Fr. *u*.

a) = OD. *jū.*

ME.	OD.	NE.
ccūse	*əkjūz*	sccuso
mūsen	*əmjūz*	amuse
ūe	*djū*	due
ūke	*djūk*	duke
xcūsen	*ekskjūz*	excuse
īse, jūce	*džjəs* (*džūs*)	juice
ūsike	*mjūzik*	musice
rūdence	*prjūdəns* (*prūdəns*)	prudence
efūsen	*rifjūz*	refuse
īde	*rjūd* (*rūd*)	rude
s	*jūs*	use.

b) = OD. *ū* after *r, š, dž.*

ME.	OD.	NE.
jūse, jūce	*džūs* (*džjūs*)	juice
prūdence	*prūdəns* (*prjūdəns*)	prudence
rūde	*rūd* (*rjūd*)	rude
sūgre	*šūgər* (*šugər*)	sugar
crūél	*krūil*	cruel.

c) = OD. *ęu.*

glūe	*dlęu*	glue.

d) = OD. *u.*

sūgre	*šugər* (*šūgər*)	sugar.

ME. $\bar{u}$ = OFr. $\ddot{u}i$.

a) = OD. $j\bar{u}$.

ME.	OD.	NE.
fruit (frŭt)	frjūt	fruit
	(frūt)	
nŭisaunce	njūsəns	nuisance
pŭe	pjū	pew
pursŭe	pə^rsjū	pursue
	(pərsŭ)	
sŭite, seŭte	sjūt (sūt)	suit.

b) = OD. $\bar{u}$.

ME.	OD.	NE.
fruit (frŭt)	frūt	fruit
	(frjūt)	
pursŭe	pə^rsŭ	pursue
	(pə^rsjū)	
sŭite, seŭte	sūt	suit.
	(sjūt)	

Diphthongs.

ai (ei).

1. Spontaneous Development.

A. English Sources.

§ 34.

ME. *ai (ei)* has two developments in words of English origin: $\bar{e}$ before unvoiced consonants, $\bar{e}^i$ before voiced consonants or when final.

1. ME. *ai (ei)* = OE. $\breve{e}$ ($\breve{æ}$) + $\mathfrak{z}$.

ME.	OD.	NE.
clai	tleⁱ	clay
dai	dēⁱ (dĭ)	day
daies-ie	dēⁱzi	daisy.
gray, grey	grēⁱ	grey
hey	ēⁱ	hay
keie	kēⁱ	key

ME.	OD.	NE.
mai	mēⁱ	may
maide	mēⁱden	maiden
nail	nēⁱl	nail
nēie	nēⁱ	to neigl
plaie, pleie	plēⁱ	play
rain, rein	rēⁱn	rain
sail, seil	sēⁱl	sail
sain, sein	sēⁱ	say
way; wey, wei.	wēⁱ	way.

2. ME. *ei* before *ght* (*ght* = *ei*).

ME.	OD.	NE.
eight	ēt	eight
weight	wēt	weight.

B. French Sources.

ME. *ai (ei)* = e before unvoiced consonants, $\bar{e}^i$ before voiced consonants and final as above.

claime	tlēⁱm	claim
compleine	komplēⁱn	complain

delaye	dilēⁱ	delay
faile	fēⁱl	fail
feint	fēⁱnt	faint
maintene	mēⁱntēⁱn	maintai
obeien	obēⁱ	obey
paie	pēⁱ	pay

ME.	OD.	NE.
ainte	*pē͜ᵢnt*	paint
eine	*pē͜ᵢn*	pain
lain	*plē͜ᵢn*	plain
	(plīn)	
reie	*prē͜ᵢ*	pray
il, reil	*rē͜ᵢl*	rail
ine	*rē͜ᵢn*	rein
eile	*vē͜ᵢl*	veil
aite	*wēt*	wait.

The development is still the same before Dentals where the lit. language has ī.

ME.	OD.	NE.
eise	*ē͜ᵢz*	ease
pais	*pēs*	peace
treiten	*trēt*	treat.

Note: Sometimes the ē̜ or ē' is shortened.

C. Scandinavian Sources.

reiþ-līc	*grē͜ᵢdli*	properly, suitable
ai	*nē͜ᵢ*	nay
lei, they	*ðē͜ᵢ*	they.

Also ME. *ei* + *k* where the terary language has *ī* < *ē* (cp.

Luick, Arch. CVIII p. 327 ff. and Björkman 298):

faik	*fē͜ᵢk*	fake
kaiken	*kē͜ᵢk*	to upset
leik, laik	*lē͜ᵢk*	to play
stayke	*stē͜ᵢk*	steak
weik, waik	*wē͜ᵢk*	weak.

Note: ME. *ai*, *ei* (from various sources) > *ī*, *īə*.

naine	*tšīen*	chain
	(tšen)	
ai	*dī (dē͜ᵢ)*	day
ie	*lī*	lay

leide	*līd*	laid
lezen	*līn*	lain
plain	*plīn*	plain.
	(plē͜ᵢn)	

2. Development in Combination.

§ 35.

ME. *ai* (*ei*) + *r* = *ə̄ʳ*.

eire	*əfə̄ʳ*	affair
iaire	*tšə̄ʳ (tšīə̄ʳ)*	chair
ierie	*də̄ri*	dairy
	(də̄͜ᵢri)	

feire	*fə̄ʳ*	fair
maire	*mə̄(ə)ʳ*	mayor
peir	*pə̄ʳ*	pair
steir	*stə̄ʳz*	stairs
	(stīə̄ʳz)	
theire	*ðə̄ʳ*	their.

au.

1. Spontaneous Development.

A. English Sources.

§ 36.

ME. *au* appears in the OD. as $\bar{\varrho}$.

ME.	OD.	NE.
lawe	$l\bar{\varrho}$	law
sawe	$s\bar{\varrho}$	saw.

1. ME. *au* = OE. *a* + ȝ.

ME.	OD.	NE.
drawe	$dr\bar{\varrho}$	draw
gnawe	$n\bar{\varrho}$	gnaw
hawe + þorn	$\bar{\varrho}þ\bar{o}^rn$	hawthorn

2. ME. *au* = OE. *a, ea +*

raw	$r\bar{\varrho}$	raw
thawe	$þ\bar{\varrho}$	thaw.

B. French Sources.

1. ME. *au* = Fr. *au.*

auter	$\bar{\varrho}te^r$	altar
autour	$\bar{\varrho}þə^r$	author
autumpne	$\bar{\varrho}təm$	autumn
cause	$k\bar{\varrho}z$	cause.

2. ME. *au* (*a*) = Fr *a* + Nasal > $\bar{\varrho}$.

avauntage	$ədv\bar{\varrho}ntid\check{z}$	advantage
aunt	$\bar{\varrho}nt$ ($\bar{e}^{\prime}nt$)	aunt
braunche	$br\bar{\varrho}nt\check{s}$	branch
change	$t\check{s}\bar{\varrho}nd\check{z}$*	change
dauncen	$d\bar{\varrho}ns$ (*dains*)	dance
daunger	$d\bar{\varrho}nd\check{z}ə^r$*	danger
straunge	$str\bar{\varrho}nd\check{z}$*	strange.

* Note: These forms sometimes appear with $\check{o}$.

3. In other cases *au* + has given *aindž* (cp. Luick, An 16, p. 480):

aungel	*aindžel*	angel
araungen	*əraindž*	arrange

4. The following French w have $\check{o}$ for *a(u)*.

auncestres	*onsete'z*	ancesto
braunche	*bronts* (*br\bar{\varrho}nt\check{s}*)	branch
chaump- ioun	*t\check{s}ompjən*	champi
chaunce	*t\check{s}ons*	chance
dauncen	*dons* (*dains, d\bar{\varrho}ns*)	dance
graunt	*gron*	graunt
laumpe	*lomp*	lamp.

2. Development in Combination.

§ 37.

1. ME. *au* before *ght* = *au*.

ME.	OD.	NE.
ıght	*aut*	aught
raught	*draut*	draught
aught	*naut*	naught
aughty	*nauti*	naughty
aughter	*slautə^r*	slaughter.

gh > *f* in the form *lauf* or *lē^if* = "laugh" (ME. laughen, OE. lahhan (cp. Luick, "Anglia" 16, . 474 and 492 ff.).

2. ME. *au* before *f, v* = *ē* or *ę^i*.

ME.	OD.	NE.
sauf	*sē^if*	safe
sauve	*sē^iv*	save.

Note: also *lē^if* = *laugh* < ME. *lauʒhe* < OE. *hlæhhan*; cp. Horn, Unters. p. 18.

3. ME. *au* = *a*, however, in:

sauvage	*savidž*	savage.

ọu.

1. Spontaneous Development.

§ 38.

ME. ọu (ōw) = ọ.

1. ME. ọu (ọw) = OE. ẹo + *w*.

ME.	OD.	NE.
lōwe, blēwe	*blǫ*	blow
Note:)w^• ,	*jō* (stressed) *jǒ* (un-stressed)	} you.

2. ME. ọu (ọw) = OE. ọ + *w*.

ME.	OD.	NE.
flọwe	*flǭ*	flow
rọwe	*rǭ*	row
Note:		
grọwe	*grǖ*	grow.

2. Development in Combination.

§ 39.

ME. ọu + *r* = ǭə^r.

ur	*fǭə^r*	four

Note:

| (ēower) yūre | *jǭ^r* (unstr) *jǭə^r* (stressed) | } your. |

4

ǫu.

1 Spontaneous Development.

§ 40.

I. ME. $\bar{ǫ}u$ = OD. $\bar{ǫ}$.

1. ME. $\bar{ǫ}u$ ($\bar{ǫ}w$) = OE. $a + w$.

ME.	OD.	NE.
blǭwe	blǭ	blow
crǫ̈we	krǭ	crow
knǫ̈we	nǭ	know
slǭw	slǭ	slow
snǭw	snǭ (snū)	snow
sǭwe	sǭ	sow
thrǭwe	þrǭ	throw.

2. ME. $\bar{ǫ}u$ ($\bar{ǫ}w$) = OE. $\bar{a} + ʒ$.

ǭwen	ǭn	own.

3. ME. $\bar{ǫ}u$ ($\bar{ǫ}w$) = OE. $\breve{o} + ʒ$.

bǭwe	bǭ	bow.

II. ME. $\bar{ǫ}u$ = OD. au i the following.

ME.	OD.	NE.
lǭw	lau	low
mǭwe	mau (mū, muf)	mow
sǭule	saul	soul.

III. ME. $\bar{ǫ}u$ = $\bar{u}$ in th following.

mǭwe	mū (mau, mow muf)	
snǫ̈we	snū (snǭ)	snow.

2. Development in Combination.

§ 41.

1. ME. $\bar{ǫ}u + gh$ = auf.

coughe	kauf	cough
dough	dauf	dough
tough	tauf	tough
trough	trauf	trough.

2. ME. $\bar{ǫ}u + ght$ = aut. (= OE. oh).

bougthe	baut	bought
brought	braut	brought
doughter	dautər	daughter
drought	draut	drought
fought	faut	fought
soughte	saut	sought
thoughte	þaut	thought.

ęu.

1. Spontaneous Development.

§ 42.

ME. *ęu* = OD. *jū* or *ū*, after
d = *džū*.

   I. ME. *ęu* = OE. *ēaw.*

   a) = OD. *jū.*

ME.	OD.	NE.
dęw	džū	dew
fęwe	fjū	few
hęwe	hjū	hew.

b) = OD. *ū.*

ME.	OD.	NE.
schręwe	šrū	shrew.

   c) = OD. *ǭ.*

schęwe (ou)	šǭ	show.

    II. ME. *ęu* = OE. *eow* =
OD. *jū.*

ęwe	jū	ewe.

ęu.

1. Spontaneous Development.

A. English Sources.

§ 43.

ME. *ęu* > OD. *ęu, jū, ū.*
   1. ME. *ęu* = OE. *ēow.*
   a) = OD. *ęu.*

ME.	OD.	NE.
blęw	blęu	blew
bręwe	bręu (brū)	brew
chęwe	tšęu	chew
clęwe	tlęu	clue
gręw	gręu (grū)	grew
tręuthe	tręuþ	truth.

   b) = OD. *jū.*

knęw	njū	knew

ME.	OD	NE.
nęwe	njū	new
ęw	jū	yew.

   c) = OD. *ū*, mostly after *r* as
a byeform with *ęu.*

bręwe	brū (bręu)	brew
gręw	grū (gręu)	grew
ręwe	rū	rue.

   2. ME. *ęu* = OE. *īw* =
OD. *jū.*

spęwe	spjū	spew.

B. French Sources.

   1. ME. *ęu* = Fr. *eu* = OD.
ęu and *ū.*

   a) = OD. *ęu.*

blęw	blęu	blue
ręule	ręul	rule.

b) = OD. *ū* after *r.*

Hebręu	ībrū	Hebrew.

   2. ME. *ęu* = Fr. *iu* =
OD. *ū.*

Jęw	Džū	Jew.

4*

oi (ui).

1. Spontaneous Development.

§ 44.

Nearly all the words in *oi* (*ui*) in ME. come from Old French In the OD. this sound is represented either by *oi* or *əi*. Cp. Luick "Anglia" 14, 294 ff.

A. French Sources.

1. ME. *oi* (*ui*) = Fr. *oi* (*ui*).

a) = OD. *oi*.

ME.	OD.	NE.
anoye, anuye	*ənoi*	annoy
apointen	*əpoint*	appoint
avoide	*əvoid*	avoid
coin	*koin*	coin
coi	*koi*	coy
emploien	*imploi*	employ
joie	*džoi*	joy
moiste	*moist*	moist
oinement	*ointmənt*	ointment
poise, peise	*poiz*	to kick
rejoissen	*ridžois*	rejoice
toilen	*toil*	toil (vb).

b) = OD. *oi* or *əi*.

broile	*broil, brəil*	broil
choise	*tšois, tšeis*	choice
disapointen	*dizəpoint, dizəpəint*	disapoint
destruien	*distroi, distrəi*	destroy
joint	*dzoint, dzəint*	joint

ME.	OD.	NE.
noise	*noiz, nəiz*	noise
oile	*oil, əil*	oil
oistre	*oistəʳ, əisdəʳ*	oyster
point	*point, pəint*	point
spoile	*spəil*	spoil
vois	*vois, vəis*	voice.

c) = OD. *əi*.

boile, boyle	*bəil*	boil
joine	*dzəin*	join
puisoun	*pəizn*	poison.

2. ME. *oi* from other French Sources.

OD. *oi* or *əi*.

loine (OF. logne, MF. longe)	*loin, ləin*	loin
soile (OF. soel, MF. sueil)	*soil, səil*	soil (sb).

B. ME. *oi* from Non-French Sources.

boie	*boi*	boy
boistrous	*boistərəs*	boisterous
loiteren	*loitəʳ*	loiter.

C. OD. *oi* from Unknown Sources.

ME.	OD.	NE.	ME.	OD.	NE.
boi	buoy		*toi*	toy.
foist, fɔist	to stink[1]			

SECTION II.

THE SHORTENING IN THE OLDHAM DIALECT OF ME. LONG VOWELS AND DIPHTHONGS.

ē.

§ 45.

1. ME. *ē* has been shortened during the ME. period in the following.

a) ME. *e* = OE. *æ* and *ē.*

ME.	OD.	NE.
edder	*eddər*	adder
het	*het*	named
leste	*les*	lest.

b) ME. *e* = OE. *ęa.*

ME.	OD.	NE.
bet	bet (bjet)	beaten
flę-	flek (fleik)	flea
shrede	*šred*	shred.

c) ME. = OE. *ēo.*

ME.	OD.	NE.
bent	*bent*	coarse grass.

2. ME. *ę̄* = OE. *ęa (ai + i, j)* = shortened OD. *ĕ.*

ME.	OD.	NE.
chę̄p	*tšep (tšĭəp)*	cheap
drę̄m	*drem (drīəm)*	dream
lę̄d	*led*	lead (sb)

ME.	OD.	NE.
rę̄d	*red*	red
þrę̄t	*þret*	threat.

3. ME. *ę̄* = OE. *æ (ai + i, j).*

ME.	OD.	NE.
clę̄ne	*tlen (tlīən)*	clean
rę̄di	*redi*	ready.

4. Also the following ME. *ę̄* from French Sources.

ME.	OD.	NE.
fę̄saunt	*feznt*	pheasant
plę̄se	*plez (plīez)*	please
plę̄süre	*plezər*	pleasure
rę̄soun	*rezn*	reason.

5. ME. *ę̄* = OE. *ęo* = OD. *ĕ.*

ME.	OD.	NE.
brę̄st	*brest*	breast
frę̄nd	*frend*	friend.

6. ME. *ę̄ — ę̄* = OE. *æ* from. W. G. *a* = OD. *ĕ.*

ME.	OD.	NE.
drę̄de	*dred*	dread.

7. ME. *ē* (Medium *e*) = OE. *ё* in open syllables = OD. *ĕ* (perhaps OE. *ĕ* preserved).

ME.	OD.	NE.
frę̄te	*fret*	fret
knę̄de	*ned (nīed)*	knead.

---

[1] Cp. NED., and Horn, Untersuchungen, p. 91.

Ī.

§ 46.

ME.	OD.	NE.
Whītstāre	*hwitstər*	bleacher
wīnberi	*wimbri*	bilberry
hwītsundei	*Wissən*	Whit-sunday.

ME. *ī* = *ĭ* in the OD.

Note: OE. *īc* = ME. *ī* a special development in the O having become *ǭ* in accented ε *ă* in unaccented positions.

Ǭ.

§ 47.

ME. *ǭ* has been shortened to *o* in the following.

ME.	OD.	NE.
*brǭken	*brok(n)*	broken
cǭmb	*kom*	comb
hǭlidāi	*holidi*	holiday

ME.	OD.	NE.
*ǭpen	*opn*	open
*spǭken	*spokn*	spoken
tǭken	*tokn*	token
*(weven) wǭven	*wov(n)*	woven.

* Original *ŏ* seems to be preserved in above.

Ō.

§ 48.

1. ME. *ō* > *u* has been shortened to *ŭ* in the following (cp. also § 29, 3).

ME.	OD.	NE.
blōd	*blud*	blood
bōsum	*buzm*	bosom
brōđer	*brudər*	brother
dōn	*dun (dṇn)*	done
flōd	*flud*	flood
gōd	*gud*	good
glōve	*dluv*	glove

ME.	OD.	NE.
hōd	*hud*	hood
stōd	*stud*	stood
twōpens	*tupens*	twopence

2. ME. *ō* has been shorten to *ŏ* (in the ME. period) in:

ME.	OD.	NE.
ōther	*odər*	other
Mōnendai	*Mondi*	Monday
fodder	*fodər*	fodder,

$\bar{u}$.

§ 49.

ME. $\bar{u}$ has been shortened to u in the following (before m, n and $\eta = u$).

ME.	OD.	NE.
croume	krṵm	crumb
crūnen	krṵnə^r	coroner
	(krṵnə^r)	
dūke	duk	duck
dūve	duv	dove
grūnd	grṵn	ground
	(grṵnd)	
hūswif	huẕi	hussy
ploume	plṵm	plum

ME.	OD.	NE.
pouke	puk	puck
schouve	šuv	shove
scūm	skṵm	scum
souke	suk	suck
sūpen	sup	sup-, drink
þūme	þum	thumb
ūle + let	ulə^{r}t	owlet.

Note: ME. $\bar{u}$ has been preserved as $\bar{u}$ in:

ME.	OD.	NE.
rough	rūf	rough
inough	ənūf	enough.

ai (ei).

§ 50.

In the following words ME. *ai (ei)* has been shortened to *e*.

ME.	OD.	NE.
agein	əgen	again
ageinest	əgen	against

ME.	OD.	NE.
chaine	tšen(tšīən)	chain
plaise	plez	please
saide	sed	said
seies	sez	says.

SECTION III.

SUMMARY OF THE ME. VOWELS IN COMBINATION.

I. Vowels before *l*.

§ 51.

1. Before *l* final.

ME.	OD.	NE.
$a > \rho$ (*l* dropped).		
ıl	ρ	all.
$o > ou$ (*l* dropped).		
ol	tou	toll,

ME.	OD.	NE.
$u > \bar{u}$ (*l* dropped).		
ful	fū	full.
$\breve{o} > au$.		
sǫle	saul	sole.

Note: For $\bar{\rho} > oi$ cp. § 27, IV.

2. Before *l* + Consonant.

a) Before *ld*.

u > *ū* with dropping of *l*.

ME.	OD.	NE.
schulder	*šūdə^r*,	shoulder.
	šūdə^r	
	(*šilde^r*)	

ǭ > *au* with dropping of *l*.

| bōld | *baud* | bold. |

b) Before *lt*.

a > *ǭ* with dropping of *l*.

| faltren | *fǭter* | falter. |

o > *ou* with dropping of *l*.

| bolt | *bout* | bolt. |

u > *ū* with dropping of *l*.

| culter | *kūte^r* | plough-share. |

c) Before *lk*.

a > *ǭ* (*l* dropped).

| balk | *bǭk* | log of timber. |

o > *ǭ* (*l* drodped).

ME.	OD.	NE.
folc	*fǫk* (*fok*)	folk.

Note: *u* remains *u*.

| hulke | *ulk* | bulk. |

d) Before *ls*.

a > *ǭ* with dropping of *l*

| fals | *fǫs* | false. |

o > *ou* with dropping of

| bolster | *boustə^r* | bolster. |

e) Before *lf*.

a > *ǭ* with dropping of *l*

| calf | *kǭv* | calf. |

f) Before *lm*.

a > *ǭ* with dropping of *f*

| halm | *hǭm* | handle an axe |

II. Vowels before *r*.

[*ar* > *ā^r*.]

| dar | *dā^r* | dare. |

er > *ə^r*, *ə^r*, *ā^r*.

hert	*hə^rt*	heart
gers	*ge^rs*	grass
lernen	*lā^rn*	learn.

ir > a) *ə^r* in closed syllables.

| wirchen | *wə^rtš* | work (vb). |

> b) *ā^r* (rare).

| kirnel | *kā^rnel* | kernel. |

or > a) *ǭ^r*.

| ord | *ǭ^rts* | broken victuals. |

> b) *ǎ^r*.

| corn | *kā^rn* | corn. |

ur > *ǎ^r*.

| burre | *bǎ^r* | a sticky plant. |

ār > *ǎ^r* (very long).

| hāre | *hǎ^r* | hare. |

ẹr (OE. *ẹ* [*ō + i, j*]) > a) *iə^r*

| wēriȝ | *wiəri* | weary. |

> b) *ēə^r*.

| wēry | *wēə^ri* | weary. |

ẹr (OE. *ẹ* = WG. final) >

| hẹre | *iə^r* | here. |

ẹr (OE. *ẹo*) > *iə^r*.

| bẹr | *biə^r* | bear. |

ẹr before Consonant (Fr.) >

| fẹrs | *fiə^rs* | fierce. |

ẹr final (Fr.) > a) aiə̯ʳ.

ME.	OD.	NE.
ꭏuẹr	kwaiə̯ʳ	choir.

b) iə̯ʳ.

| ꞓhẹre | tšiə̯ʳ | cheer. |

ēr (ē — ḝ) (= WG. ā).
a) > iẹʳ.

| bẹre | biə̯ʳ | bier. |

b) > ə̄ʳ.

| wẹre | uə̄ʳ (wiə̯ʳ) | were. |

ẹr (Medium ē).
a) > iə̯ʳ.

| schẹre | šiə̯ʳ | shear. |

b) > ẹ̄ə̯ʳ.

| bẹre | bẹ̄ə̯ʳ | bear (sb). |

c) > ə̄ʳ.

| pẹre | pə̄ʳ (pẹ̄ə̯ʳ) | pear. |

īr > aiə̯ʳ or əiə̯ʳ.

ME.	OD.	NE.
fīr	fəiə̯ʳ	fire.

ọr > a) ūə̯ʳ.

| mọre | mūə̯ʳ | more. |

> b) ọ̄ʳ, ọ̄ə̯ʳ (scarce).

| bọren | bọ̄ʳn | born. |

ọ̄r > ūə̯ʳ.

| flọr | flūə̯ʳ | floor. |

ūr > ẹūə̯ʳ.

| flour | fleūə̯ʳ (flə̄ʳ) | flower. |

air (eir) > ə̄ʳ (iə̯ʳ).

| steir | stə̄'z (stiə̯ʳz) | stairs. |

our > ọ̄ə̯ʳ.

| four | fọ̄ə̯ʳ | four. |

III. Vowels before m, n, ŋ.

a > o (except when w precedes).

ram	rom	ram
man	mon	man
ranc	roŋk	rank.

o > u before ŋ.

| belongen | biluŋg | belong. |

au > ai before ndž.

| aungel | aindžel | angel. |

e > i before ŋg, ndž.

| English | iŋgliš | English |
| henge | indž | hinge. |

IV. Vowels before gh.

au > ē^i.

| laughen | lē^if | laugh. |

ou > a) au, ū, u (with change of gh to f or loss thereof).

tough	tauf	tough
rough	rū, rūf	rough
slough	sluf, slau	slough.

o > ọ̄, au.

| trogh | trọ̄f, trauf | trongh. |

χt > īt.

| bright | brīt | bright. |

quχt > aut.

| fought | faut | fought. |

V. Vowels before f, v.

au > a) ē, ē^i.

| sauf | sē^if | safe. |
| sauve | sē^iv | save. |

> b) a.

| sauvage | savidž | savage. |

VI. Vowels before š.

ai > ai.

ME.	OD.	NE.
dasshe	*daiš*	dash.

Note: For *e < a* before š cp. § 4, 5.

i > ī.

fisch	*fiš*	fish.

Note: I have not come across the change *u > yǐ* before š noted by Hargreaves (§ 34, c, Note) in the OD.

ü > u.

ME.	OD.	NE.
prüssche	*þruš*	thrush.

Appendix to Chapter II.

Sources of the Oldham Vowels.

I. Short Vowels.

a.

§ 52.

1. Oldham a mostly corresponds to ME. *a.*

1. ME. *a.*

a) OE. *a* (§ 3, A, a, 1) *arə* arrow, *ban* curse, *gam* game.

b) OE. *æ* (§ 3, A, a, 2) *baliz* bellows, *daft* silly, *rafðər* rafte

c) OE. *ea* (§ 3, A, a, 3) *galəsiz* braces, *narə* narrow.

d) OE. *ă* (§ 3, A, b) *aks* ask, *atðərkrop* spider.

e) OE. *æ* (§ 3, A, c) *ani* any, *laddər* ladder, *mad* mad angry.

f) OE. *ēa* (§ 3, A, d) *tšap* chap, *tšafər* (to) haggle, *ladər* (*lodə* lather.

g) Scand. *a* (§ 3, B) *farəntli* handsomely, *kaŋk* (*koŋk*) gossiping conversation.

h) Celtic *a* (§ 3, C) *brat* coarse apron, *kamd* cross-tempere

i) French *a* (*ã*) in open syllables, unaccented in OFr. (AFr (§ 3, D, a) *barəl* barrel, *damidž* damage, *pariš* parish.

j) French *a* (*ã*) in closed syllables unaccented in OFr. (AFr (§ 3, D, b) *katš* catch, *manti* mantle.

k) French *a* (*ā*) in closed syllables accented in OFr. (AFr.)
(§ 3, **D**, c) *ant* aunt, *tšans* (*tšons*) chance.

2. ME. *au.*

a) French *au* (§ 37, 3) *savidž* savage.

e.

§ 53.

Oldham *e* in most cases corresponds to ME. *e.*

1. ME. *e.*

a) OE. *e, eo* (§ 5, A, a) *betđə^r* better, *frem* not akin, *wentš* girl.

b) Scand. *e* (§ 5, B) *deg* cut off, *feli* fellow.

c) French *ę, ę̆, ē̆,* accented, (§ 5, C, a) *lekšən* election, *fent* remnant of cloth.

d) French *ę, ę̆, ē̆,* secondary accent, (§ 5, C, b) *bebridž* beverage.

e) OE. *a* (§ 6, 2) *weš* wash, (§ 4, 5) *es* ashes.

2. ME. *i* before *r* in open syllables.

a) OE. *y* (§ 8, 1, b) *beri* bury, *werit* (*wə^rit*) worry.

b) Fr. *y* (§ 7, C, b) *serəp* syrup.

[c) Fr. *e* (§ 7, C, b) *sperit* spirit.]

3. ME. *ē̆.*

a) OE. *æ, ē̆* (§ 45, 1, a) *eđđə^r* adder, *les* lest.

b) OE. *ę̄a* (§ 45, 1, b) *bet* beaten, *flek* flea.

c) OE. *ēo* (§ 45, 1, c) *bent* coarse grass.

d) OE. *ę̄a* (*au* + *i, j*) (§ 45, 2) *tšep* cheap, *drem* dream.

e) OE. *ǣ* (*ai* + *i, j*) (§ 45, 3) *tlen* clean, *redi* ready.

f) Fr. *ai* (§ 45, 4) *feznt* pheasant, *plezə^r* pleasure.

4. ME. *ę̄.*

a) OE. *ę̄o* (§ 45, 5) *brest* breast, *frend* friend.

5. ME. *ę̄ — ę̆.*

a) OE. *æ* from WG. *ā* (§ 45, 6) *dred* dread.

6. ME. *ę̄* (medium *e*).

a) OE. *ē̆* in open syllables (§ 45, 7) *fret* fret, *ned* knead.

7. ME. *ai* (*ei*) (§ 50).

    a) OE. *e* + *ʒ* *əgen* again, against.
    b) OE. *œ* + *ʒ* *sed* said, *sez* says.
    c) Fr. *ai* *tšen* chain, *plez* please.

i.

§ 54.

Oldham *i* mostly corresponds to ME. *i.*

1. ME. *i.*

    a) OE. *i* (§ 7, A, a) *brid* bird, *wik* lively, *kist* chest.
    b) OE. *y* (§ 7, A, b) *bizi* busy, *mitš* much, *šhildə^r* shoulder.
    c) Scand. *i* (§ 7, B) *blinkə^rt* blind of one eye, *kipə^r* amorous.
    d) Scand. *y* (§ 7, B) *big* build, *klink* a blow.
    e) Fr. *i*, *ī* (§ 7, C) *džilivə^r* gilly flower, *nifl* to be fastidious.

2. ME. *u.*

    a) OE. *u* (§ 12, 2) *šildə^r* shoulder.

3. ME. *ę̄.*

    a) OE. *ęo* (§ 18, 3, d) *divl* devil, *sik* sick.

4. ME. *ę̆* — *ę̄.*

    a) OE. *ę̄*, *æ* (§ 20, e) *istid* instead, *ridl* riddle.

5. ME *ī.*

    a) OE. *ȳ* (§ 25, 2, d) *litl* little, *þimbl* thimble.
    b) OE. *ī* (§ 46) *wimbri* billerry, *Wissən* Whitsunday.

o.

§ 55.

Oldham *o* mostly corresponds to ME *o.*

1. ME.

    a) OE. *o* (§ 9, A, a) *brosn* burst, *kroft* field.
    b) OE. *eo* (§ 9, A, c) *jon(d)* yonder.
    c) Scand. *o* (§ 9, B) *glopn* astonish.
    d) Other Teutonic Sources (§ 9, C) *lolopin* awkward, *nokəlz* knuckles.

e) French ǫ (o) (accented) (§ 9, D, a) *komikəl* comical, *rokit* au outer garment.

f) French ǫ (o) (unaccented) (§ 9, D, b) *konsēt* conceit, *os* try.

g) Celtic *o* (§ 9, E) *bob* to dance about, *fog* grass after mowing.

2. ME. *a*.

a) OE. *ēa* (§ 3, 1, d) *loðər* lather.

b) OE. *a* before *m, n, ŋ* (§ 4, 4) *mon* man, *rom* ram.

c) Fr. *a* before *m, n, ŋ* (§ 4, 4) *ploŋk* plank.

3. ME. *u*.

a) OE. *u* (§ 11, E, Note) *kom* (*kum*) come, *sombri* sombody.

b) Fr. *u* (§ 11, E, Note) *komfərt* (*kumfərt*) comfort.

4. ME. *ę̄*.

a) OE. *ǣ* [Germ. *ai* + *i, j*] (§ 16, 2, d) *swot* sweat.

5. ME. *ǭ*.

a) OE. *ā* (§ 27, III) *wom* (*wum*) home, *wot* hot.

b) OE. *o* (§ 47) *broken* broken, *opn* open.

6. ME. *au* (*a*) (§ 36, b, 4).

a) Fr. *a brontš* (*brǭnts*) branch. *strondž* (*strǭndž*) strange.

7. ME. *ǭ̇*.

a) ME. *ǭ̇* (§ 48, 2) *oðər* other, *Mondi* Monday.

U.

§ 56.

Oldham *u* mostly corresponds to ME. *u*.

1. ME. *u*.

a) OE. *u* (§ 11, A, 1) *butðər* butter, *kubərt* cupboard.

b) OE. *y* (§ 11, A, 2) *krutš* crutch, *šut* shut.

c) Scand. *u* (§ 11, B) *pufl* to breathe with difficulty.

d) Other Teutonic Sources (§ 11, C) *slut* a slovenly woman.

e) French *u* (*ou*) (§ 11, D) *bulš* bulge, *muz* month.

f) Celtic *u* (§ 11, E) *krud* curds.

2. ME. *ü*.

a) OE. *y* (§ 13, A) *þruš* thrush.

b) French *u* (§ 13, B) *džust* just, *studi* study.

3. ME. ọ̄ (§ 29, 3) *buk (būk)* book, *luk (lūk)* look.

    a) OE. ọ̄ (§ 48, 1) *blud* blood, *stud* stood.

    b) OE. ā (§ 48, 1) *tupəns,* twopence.

4. ME. ū.

    a) OE. ū (§ 49) *duv* dove, *šuv* shove.

    b) OE. ŭ (§ 49) *grun* ground.

    c) Sc. ū (§ 49) *puk* puck.

    d) A.-French *u* (§ 49) *krunə^r (krụnə^r)* coroner.

5. ME. ū̃.

    a) Fr. *u* (§ 33, d) *šugə (šūgə^r)* sugar.

u̞.

§ 57.

Oldham *u̞* corresponds mostly to ME. *u* before *m, n, ŋ.*

1. ME. *u.*

    a) OE. *u* (§ 11, A, 1) *ku̞mn* come (ppl.)., *dru̞ŋken* drun

    b) OE. *y* (§ 11, A, 2) *bu̞ndl* bundle [cp. Arch. 106, p.

    c) Other Teutonic Sources (§ 11, C) *plu̞mp* straight to
       point.

    d) French *o* (§ 11, D) *gu̞m* gum, *su̞m* sum.

2. ME. *ü.*

    a) OE. *y* (§ 13, A) *bu̞ndl* bundle.

    b) Fr. *u* (§ 13, B) *u̞mbl* humble, *pu̞niš* punish.

3. ME. ọ̄.

    a) OE. ā (§ 27, III) *wu̞l* whole, *wu̞ts* oats.

4. ME. ọ̄ (§ 48).

    a) OE. ọ̄ *du̞n* done.

5. ME. *o* before *ŋ.*

    a) OE. *a* (§ 10, 2) *əlu̞ŋg* along, *lu̞ŋg* long.

    [b) Sc. *e* (§ 10, 2) *du̞ŋg* struck.]

6. ME. *a* before *m, n, ŋ.*

    a) OE. ū (§ 49) *kru̞m* crumb, *gru̞n* ground.

    b) Scand. ū (§ 49) *sku̞m* scum.

    c) AFr. *a* (§ 49) *kru̞nə^r* coroner.

ǝ.

§ 58.

Oldham ǝ corresponds mostly to ME. *i* before *r* in closed syllables.

1. ME. *i* before *r* (§ 8, 1).

   a) OE. *y bǝʳl* (*bǝ̄ʳl*) to pour out, *wǝ̄ʳtš* work (vb).
   b) Scand. *y bǝ̆ʳ* velocity, force.
   c) Fr. *u ŏ̆ʳt* hurt, *pǝ̆ʳdž* purge.

2. ME. *e* before *r* final or in closed syllables.

   a) OE. *æ* (§ 6, b) *gǝʳs* grass.
   b) Fr. *e* (§ 6, b) *jǝʳst* hearse, *tǝrǝbl* terrible.

3. ME. *o* before *r* (§ 10, 1, b).

   a) OE. *o* (*h*)ǝ̆ʳn horn, *mǝʳp̄* a great quantity.
   b) Fr. *o kǝrel* coral.

4. ME. *u* before *r* (§ 12, 1).

   a) OE. *y wǝrit* (*werit*) worry.
   b) Scand. *u bǝ̆ʳ* a sticky plant.

II. Long Vowels.

ā.

§ 59.

Oldham *ā* mostly corresponds to ME. *e* before *r*.

1. ME. *e* (§ 6, 1 c).

   a) OE. *a kāʳ* low-lying marsh.
   b) OE. *ea dāʳk* blind, (*h*)āʳk listen.
   c) OE. *e skāʳ* a rocky place, *stāʳt*.
   d) OE. *eo kāʳv* (*kǝ̄ʳv*) carve, *lāʳn* learn, teach.
   e) Fr. *e sāʳtin* certain, *māʳsi* mercy.

2. ME. *i* before *r* (§ 8, 1, c).

   a) OE. *i p̄āʳd* third, *p̄āʳti* thirty.
   b) OE. *y kāʳnel* kernel.

3. ME. ę before *r* (§ 24).

    a) OE. *æ jáʳli* early.

4. ME. *a* + final *s* (§ 4, 6, Note 2).

    a) OE. *a dlās* glass, *lās* lass.

Note: The above are also found with *ă*.

ē.

§ 60.

Oldham *ē* mostly corresponds to ME. *ā* when final or before
voiced consonants.

1. ME. *ā*.

    a) OE. *a* (§ 14, A, a, 1) *ēk* ache, *hēt* hate.

    b) OE. *ea* (§ 14, A, b) *gēt* gate.

    c) OE. *æ* (§ 14, A, c) *mēpl* maple, *wēt(d)əʳ* water.

    d) Scand. *a* (§ 14 B) *gēp* gape, *gēt* way, road.

    e) Fr. *a* (§ 14, C) *bēkn* bacon, *fēs* face.

2. ME. *ę̄*.

    a) OE. *ę̄a* (§ 16, A, 1, c) *ēstəʳ* (*ēsþeʳ*) Easter, *grēt* great

    b) OE. *æ* (§ 16, A, 2, b) *sē* sea, *tētš* teach.

    c) Fr. *ai, ei* (§ 16, B, I) *ēz* ease, *ēgl* eagle, *ēgəʳ* eager.

    d) Fr. *e* (§ 16, B, II a) *disēv* deceive, *prēts* preach.

        Fr. *e* (§ 18, B, 5, c) *obēdiənt* obedient, *spēšl* special.

3. ME. *ę̄*.

    a) OE. *ę̄o* (§ 18, A, 3, c) *dël* devil, *lēf* lief.

    b) OE. *e* (§ 18, A, 5, b) *fēlt* field.

4. ME. *ę̄* — *ę̄* from W. Germ. *a*.

    a) (§ 20 A, 1, c) *spētš* speech.

5. ME. Medium *ē* = OE. *ĕ* in open syllables.

    a) OE. *ĕ* (§ 22, b) *brēk* break, *spēk* speak.

6. ME. *ai, ei* before unvoiced consonants.

    a) OE. (§ 34, A, 2) *ēt* eight.

    b) Scand. *æ wēt* weight.

    c) Fr. *ai* (§ 34, B) *wēt* wait, *trēt* treat.

7. ME. *au* before *f*.

    a) Fr. *au* (§ 37, 2) *sēf* safe.

Ī.

§ 61.

Oldham *ī* mostly corresponds to ME. *ę̄*.

1. **ME. *ę̄* (from all sources).**

   a) OE. *ę̄, ǣ* (§ 18, A, 1, a) *fīd* feed, *gīs* geese.
   b) OE. *ę̄* (§ 18, A, 2, a) *ī* he, *wī* we.
   c) OE. *ę̄o* (§ 18, A, 3, a) *dīp* deep, *þīf* thief.
   d) OE. *ę̄ (ea + i)* (§ 18, A, 4, a) *šīt* sheet, *stīpə* steeple.
   e) OE. *ĕ* (§ 18, A, 5, a) *fīlt* field, *jīld* yield.
   f) Fr. *ę́* (§ 18, B, 1) *əgrī* agree, *līdžənd* legend.
   g) Fr. *ie* (§ 18, B, 2) *tšīf* chief.
   h) Fr. *e* (§ 18, B, 5) *digrī* degree.

2. **ME. *i + ght (χt)* (§ 8, 2).**

   a) OE. *i nīt* night, *rīt* right.
   b) OE. *eo lītnin* lightening, *brīt* bright.
   c) OE. *y: frītn* frighten.

3. **ME. *i + š* (§ 8, 3).**

   a) OE *i dīš* dish, *fīš* fish.
   b) OE. *ȳ wīš* wish.

4. **ME. *ę̄*.**

   a) OE. *ę̄a* (§ 16, A, 1, b) *īst* east, *stīp* steep.
   b) OE. *ǣ* (§ 16, A, 2, c) *sī* sea.
   c) French *ai* (§ 16, B, I, c) *fīt* feat, *plīd* plead.
   d) Fr. *e* (§ 16, B, II, c) *əpīl* appeal, *sīs* cease.

5. **ME. *ę̄ — ē̦* from WG. *ā*.**

   a) OE. *ē* (§ 20, A, 1, b) *grīdi* greedy, *sīd* seed.

6. **ME. Medium *ē̆*.**

   a) OE. *ĕ* (§ 22, c) *brīkfəst* breakfast, *līt* let.

7. **ME. *ĭ*.**

   a) OE. *ȳ* (§ 25, A, 2, c) *tīn* shut, *wīs* wish.

5

8. ME. *ai, ei* (§ 34, Note).
   a) OE. *æ* + *ʒ* *dī* day.
   b) OE. *e* + *ʒ* *līd* laid, *lī* lay.
   c) Fr. *ai* *plīn* plain.

$\bar{Q}.$

§ 62.

Oldham *ǭ* mostly corresponds to ME. *o*.

1. ME. *o* before *r* (§ 10, 1, a).
   a) OE. *o* *mǭʳn* morning, *ǭʳts* broken victuals.
   b) Fr. *o* *kwǭ'd* cord, *fǭʳtin* fortune.
2. ME. + NE final *l* (§ 4, 1, Note).
   a) OE. *a, ea*: *ǭ* all, *kǭ* call, *fǭ* fall.
   b) Fr. *a*: *bǭ* ball.
   The above also appear with *ǭ̇*.
3. ME. *a* + *l* before *f* (§ 4, 2), *m, k, s, t* (§ 4, 3).
   a) OE. *a, ea* *kǭv* calf, *ǭv* half.
   (*h*)*ǭm* handle of an axe, *mǭt* malt.
   b) Fr. *a*: *fǭs* sly, cunning.
4. ME. *ǭ* before *r* (§ 28, 2).
   a) OE. *o* *bǭʳn* born.
5. ME. *au*.
   a) OE. *a* + *ʒ* (§ 36, A, 1) *drǭ* draw, *lǭ* law.
   b) OE. *a, ea* + *w* (§ 36, A, 2) *rǭ* raw, *þǭ* thaw.
   c) Fr. *au* (§ 36, B, 1) *ǭtəʳ* altar, *ǭtəm* autumn.
   d) Fr. *a* + *Nasal* (§ 36, B, 2) *brǭnts* branch.

$\bar{O}.$

§ 63.

Oldham *ǭ̇* mostly corresponds to ME. *ọu*.
1. ME *ọu*.
   a) OE. *ā̤* + *w* (§ 40, I, 1) *krǭ̇* crow, *slǭ̇* slow.
   b) OE. *ā* + *ʒ* (§ 40, I, 2) *ǭ̇n* own.
   c) OE. *ŏ* + *ʒ* (§ 40, I, 3) *bǭ̇* bow.

2. ME. *a* + NE. final *l* (§ 4, 1).
 ǭ all, *kǭ* call, *fǭ* fall.
 Note: The above also appear with *ǭ*.
3. ME. *ǫ* (§ 27, II).
  a) OE. *ā* *ǝrǭz* arose, *gōt* goat.
  b) OE. *o* *hǭp* hope.
  c) Fr. *o* *brǭtš* broach, *nǭtis* notice.
4. ME. *ǫu*.
  a) OE. *ēo* + *w* (§ 38, 1) *blǭ* blow.
  b) OE. *ō* + *w* (§ 38, 2) *flǭ* flow, *rǭ* row.
5. ME. *o* + *lk* (§ 10, 3, b).
  a) OE. *o* *fǭk* (*fok*) folk.
  b) OE. *eo* *jǭk* yolk.

ū (*jū*).

§ 64.

Oldham *ū* mostly corresponds to ME. *ǭ*.
1. ME. *ǭ*.
  a) OE. *ǭ* (§ 29, A, 1, a) *brūm* broom, *dū* do.
  b) OE. *ā* (§ 29, A, 1, b) *hū* who, *wūm* womb.
  c) Fr. *o* (§ 29, B) *ǝprūv* approve, *mūv* move.
2. ME. *u* + *l* final or before *l*, *d*, *t* (§ 12, 2).
  a) OE. *u* *kūtǝr* ploughshare, *pū* pull.
  b) Scand. *u* *būdǝr* boulder.
3. ME. *ē* (§ 18, A, 3, e).
  a) OE. *ēo* *djūl* devil.
4. ME. *ū*.
  a) Fr. *u* (§ 33, B, I, a and b) *džūs* juice, *jūs* use.
  b) Fr. *üi* (§ 33, B, II a and b) *frūt* fruit, *sjūt* suit.
5. ME. *ǫu* (rare).
  a) OE. *ǭ* (§ 38, 2, Note) *grū* grow.
6. ME. *ǫu* (§ 40, 3).
  a) OE. *ā* + *w* *mū* mow, *snū* snow.

5*

7. ME. *ęu*.
   a) OE. *ęa* + *w* (§ 42, I, a and b) *fjū* few, *šrū* shrew.
   b) OE. *eow* (§ 42, II) *jū* ewe.

8. ME. *ęu*.
   a) OE. *ęow* (§ 43, A, 1, b) *njū* new, *jū* yew.
   b) OE. *ęow* after *r* (§ 43, A, 1 c) *brū* brew, *grū* grew.
      Note: These also appear with *ęu*.
   c) OE. *īw* (§ 43, A, 2) *spjū* spew.
   d) Fr. *eu* (§ 43, B, 1, b) *ībrū* Hebrew.
   e) Fr. *iu* (§ 43, B, 2) *Džū* Jew.

ə̄.

§ 65.

Oldham *ə̄* only occurs before *r*.

1. ME. *e* + *r* (§ 6, 1, a).
   a) OE. *e, eo kə̄ʳn* churn, *də̄ʳn* darn.
      bə̄ʳm barm, *hə̄ʳt* heart.

2. ME. *i* + *r* (§ 8, 1) in closed syllables.
   a) OE. *y bə̄ʳl* to pour ont, *wə̄ʳm* worm.
   b) Scand. *y bə̄ʳ* velocity, *fə̄ʳbobz* fircones.
   c) Fr. *u ə̄ʳt* hurt, *pə̄ʳdž* purge.
      Note: The above also occur with *ə̆*.

3. ME. *o* + *r* (§ 10, 1, b).
   a) OE. *o kə̄ʳn* corn, *þə̄ʳn* thorn.
   b) Fr. *o fə̄ʳtin*.

4. ME. *u* + *r* (§ 12, 1).
   a) OE. *u hə̄ʳst* wood, grove, *wə̄ʳtš* work.
   b) Scand. *u bə̄ʳ* a sticky plant, *(h)ə̄ʳ* to purr.
      Note: The above also occur with *ə̆*.

5. ME. *ā* + *r* (§ 15).
   a) GE. *a fə̄ʳ* fare, *stə̄ʳ* stare.

6. ME. *ę̄* — *ę̆* + *r* (§ 21, 2).
   a) OE. *œ wə̄ʳ* wore, *wə̄ʳ (wīə̄ʳ)* where.

7. ME. Medium $\bar{e}$ + r (§ 23, 1, c).

 a) OE. $\breve{e}$ $b\jmath^r$ bear, $p\jmath^r$ pear.

8. ME. $\bar{u}$ + r (rare) (§ 32).

 a) Fr. ou: $fl\jmath^r$ ($fl\varrho u\jmath^r$) flower.

9. ME. ai (ei) + r (§ 35).

 a) OE. $æ$ + $\mathfrak{z}$: $st\jmath^r z$ ($st\bar{\imath}\jmath^r z$) stairs.
 b) Sc. ei $d\bar{a}ri$ ($d\bar{e}'ri$) dairy, $d\jmath^r$ their.
 c) Fr. ai (ei) $f\jmath^r$ fair, $p\jmath^r$ pair.

III. Diphthongs.

ai.

§ 66.

1. ME. a + $\check{s}$ (§ 4, 5).

 a) OE. a $wai\check{s}$.
 b) OE. $æ$ $lai\check{s}$.
 c) Scand. a (?) $pai\check{s}$ to pour down.
 d) Fr. a $slai\check{s}$ slash.

2. ME. e + $\check{s}$ (§ 6, 2) (rare).

 a) OE. $æ$ $flai\check{s}$ ($flei\check{s}$) flesh, meat.

3. ME. $\bar{\imath}$ (literary influence).

 a) OE. $\bar{\imath}$ (§ 25, A, 1, b) $t\check{s}aim$ chime, $laif$ life.
  Note: In the above forms $\jmath i$ is also found.
  OE. $\imath$ (§ 25, A, 1, c) $wait$ white, $waiz$ wise. -
 b) OE. $\bar{y}$ (§ 25, A, 2, b) $bail$ bile, $praid$ pride.
 c) OE. $\bar{\imath}, y$ + $\mathfrak{z}$ (§ 25, A, 3) $stail$ stile, $tail$ tile.
 d) OE. $\bar{e}o$ + $\mathfrak{z}$ (§ 25, A, 4) lai to tell lies.
 e) Fr. i (§ 25, B, b) $fain\jmath l$ final, $paint$ pint.
  Note: In the above $\jmath i$ also found.
  Fr. i (§ 25, B, c) $dilait$ delight, $prais$ price.
 f) Scand. i (§ 25, C) $þraiv$ thrive.

4. ME. au + $nd\check{z}$, ns (§ 36, B, 3).

 a) Fr. $aind\acute{æ}l$ angel, $dains$ dance.

au.

§ 67.

Oldham au corresponds mostly to ME. *au* before *ght.*

1. ME. *au* (§ 37, 1).
   a) OE. *ā + w aut* aught.
   b) Sc. *a + h draut* draught.
2. ME. *ol* before *l, st, t* (§ 10, 3, a).
   a) OE. *o bau* bowl, *pau* to cut.
3. ME. *ǫ + l* before *d* (§ 28, 1).
   a) OE. *ā, ea bihaud* behold, *faut* fold.
   saud sold.
   b) OE. *o saul* sole.
4. ME. *ǫu* particularly before *ght* (§§ 40, II and 41, 2).
   a) OE. *ā + w* (§ 40, II) *saul* soul.
   b) OE. *oh* (§ 41, 2) *baut* bought, *dautǝʳ* daughter.

ēi (ēⁱ).

§ 68.

Oldham *ēⁱ (ei)* mostly corresponds to ME. *ā* when final or befo
unvoiced consonants.

1. ME. *ā* (§ 14, A, a, 2).
   a) OE. *a neⁱm* name, *tēⁱl* tale.
   b) OE. *ea* (§ 14, A, b) *ēⁱl* ale, *šēⁱd* shade.
   c) OE. *æ* (§ 14, a, c) *blēⁱd* blade, *rēⁱvn* raven.
   d) Sc. *a* (§ 14, B) *gēⁱz* gaze.
   e) Fr. *a* (§ 14, C) *ēⁱbl* able, *fēⁱbl* feeble.
2. ME. *e + š* (Rochdale influence) (§ 6, 2).
   a) OE. *a wĕiš* wash.
   b) OE. *æ flēiš* flesh, meat.
   c) OE. *e nĕiš* tender.
3. ME. *ę̄.*
   a) Fr. *ai* (§ 16, B, b) *ēⁱz* ease, *rēⁱzn* reason.

4. ME. *ai* (*ei*).

    a) OE. *ĕ* (*æ*) + ȝ (§ 34, A, 1) *tlĕⁱ* clay, *dĕⁱzi* daisy.

    b) Fr. *ai* (*ei*) (§ 34, B) *tlĕⁱm* claim, *obĕⁱ* obey.

    c) Sc. *ei* (§ 34, C) *grĕⁱdli* properly, suitable.

5. ME. *au* before *f*, *v* (§ 37, 2).

    a) Fr. *au* *sĕⁱv* save.

ęu.

§ 69.

Oldham *ęu* mostly corresponds to ME. *ū*.

1. ME. *ū*.

    a) OE. *ū* (§ 31, A, 1) *dęun* down, *hęus* house.

    b) OE. *ō* before *h* (§ 31, A, 2) *bęu* bough.

    c) OE. *ŭ* + ȝ (§ 31, A, 3) *fęul* fowl, *sęu* sow.

    d) Fr. *u* (*o*) before nasal (§ 31, B, 1) *əmeunt* amount.

    e) Fr. *ou* (§ 31, B, 2) *əlęu* allow, *keutš* couch.

    f) Sc. *ū* (§ 31, C) *bęun* bound, *dręup* droop.

2. ME. *ęu*.

    a) OE. *ēow* (§ 43, A, 1, a) *blęu* blew, *tręuþ* truth.

    b) Fr. *eu* (§ 43, B, 1, a) *blęu* blue.

ēə.

§ 70.

Oldham *ēə* corresponds to ME. *ē* + *r*.

1. ME. *ę̄* + *r* (§ 23, 1, b).

    a) OE. *ĕ* *bēəʳ* bear, *pēəʳ* (*pēʳ*) pear.

2. ME. *ē* + *r* (§ 19, 1, b).

    a) OE. *ę̄* + *r* *wēəri* (*wīəri*) weary.

īə.

§ 71.

Oldham *īə* mostly corresponds to ME. *ē* from various sources.

1. ME. *ę̄*.

    a) OE. *ę̄a* (§ 16, A, 1, a) *bīəm* beam, *dīəf* deaf.

    b) OE. *æ* (§ 16, A, 2, a) *tlīən* clean, *līest* least.

c) Fr. *ai* (§ 16, B, I, b) *plīəz* please, *rīəzn* reason.

Note: The above also occur with *e*.

d) Fr. *ĕ* (§ 16, B, II, b) *bīəst* beast, *resīəv* receive.

e) Fr. *ẽe* (§ 16, B, III) *sīəl* seal, *vīəl* veal.

2. ME. *ẹ̄*.

a) OE. *ẹ̄* (§ 17, A, 1, b) *brīəd* breed, *spīəd* speed.

b) OE. *ẹ̄o* (§ 17, A, 3, b) *krīəp* creep.

c) OE. *ẹ̄* (*ẹ̄a*) (§ 17, A, 4, b) *nīəd* need, *slīəv* sleeve.

d) Fr. *uẻ* (§ 17, B, 4) *bīəf* beef, *pīəpl* people.

e) Fr. *ie* (§ 17, B, 5, b) *grīəf* grief.

Fr. *ie* before *r* (§ 19, 2, 1) *fīəʳs* fierce, *pīəʳ* pier.

3. ME. *ẹ̄* — *ẹ̄* from W. Germ. *ā*.

a) OE. *ē*, *æ* (§ 20, A, 1, a) *brīəþ* breath, *slīəp* sleep.

4. ME. Medium *ē*.

a) OE. *ĕ* (§ 22, a) *nīəd* knead, *trīəd* tread.

Note: The above also appear with *ẹ̄*.

5. ME. *ai, ei* (rare) (§ 34, C, Note).

a) Fr. *ai* *tšīən* chain.

ié.

§ 72.

Oldham *ié* is only found in the single word *þiétəʳ* theatre (§ B, 3) ex ME. *thẹ̄atre*, French *théatre*.

oi.

§ 73.

Oldham *oi* mostly corresponds to ME *oi*.

1. ME. *oi*.

a) Fr. *oi* (§ 44, A, 1, a) *əpoint* appoint, *džoi* joy.

b) Fr. *o* (§ 44, A, 2, b) *loin* (*ləin*) loin.

c) Fr. *oe* (§ 44, A, 2, b) *soil* (*səil*) soil.

d) Uncertain sources (§ 44, B, c) *boi* boy, buoy.

2. ME. *o* before *l* (§ 27, IV).

a) OE. *o* *koil* (*kūəl*) coal, *oil* hole.

$\bar{\varrho}\partial$.

§ 74.

Oldham $\bar{\varrho}\partial$ mostly corresponds to ME. ϱ before final r in certain words.

1. ME. $\bar{\varrho}$ + r final (§ 28, 2).
   > Note: These words are also found with $\bar{u}\partial$.
2. ME. ou + r final (§ 39).
   a) OE. $\bar{e}o$ $f\bar{\varrho}\partial^r$ four, $j\bar{\varrho}\partial^r$ your.

$\bar{u}e$.

§ 75.

Oldham $\bar{u}e$ corresponds mostly to ME. ϱ.

1. ME. $\bar{\varrho}$.
   a) OE. a (§ 27, A, I, 1) $\partial l\bar{u}\partial n$ alone, $g\bar{u}\partial$ go.
   b) OE. o (§ 27, A, I, 2) $k\bar{u}\partial l$ ($koil$) coal, $r\bar{u}\partial z$ rose.
   c) Fr. o (§ 27, B) $k\bar{u}\partial t$ ($kwot$) coat, $r\bar{u}\partial st$ roast.
2. ME. $\bar{\varrho}$.
   a) OE. $\bar{\varrho}$ (§ 29, A, 2) $sp\bar{u}\partial n$ spoon, $tu\partial\not b$ tooth.
   b) Fr. $\bar{\varrho}$ (§ 30) $p\bar{u}\partial^r$ poor.
3. ME. $\bar{e}$ — $\bar{e}$.
   a) OE. $\bar{æ}$ (§ 20, A, 1, d) $j\bar{u}\partial^r$ hair.
4. ME. $\breve{u}$, $\bar{\varrho}$ before r.
   a) OE. u (§ 32) $d\bar{u}\partial^r$ ($d\bar{\partial}^r$) door.

$\bar{u}i$.

§ 76.

Oldham $\bar{u}i$ corresponds to:

1. ME. $\bar{u}$ + e (§ 33, B, I, e).
   a) Fr. ue $kr\bar{u}il$ cruel.
2. ME. ui (§ 44, d).
   a) Fr. ui $r\bar{u}in$ ruin, $s\bar{u}it$ suet.

əi.

§ 77.

Oldham *əi* mostly corresponds to ME. *ī*.

1. ME. *i*.

    a) OE. *ī* (§ 25, A, 1, a) *fəind* find, *məil* mile.
    b) OE. *ȳ* (§ 25, A, 2, a) *həid* hide. *məis* mice.
    c) OE. *ĭ, y* + *ʒ* (§ 25, A, 3) *drəi* dry, *təi* tie.
    d) OE. *ēa* + *ʒ* (§ 25, A, 5) *fləi* fly.
    e) OE. *ēo* + *ʒ* (§ 25, A, 4) *əi* eye.
    f) Fr. *i* (§ 25, B, a) *fəin* fine, *nəis* nice.

2. ME. *oi*.

    a) Fr. *oi* (*ui*) (§ 44, A, 1, b) *nəiz* noise, *bəil* boil.

3. ME. *i*.

    a) OE. *i* (§ 7, a) *tšəilt* (*tšilt*) child.

IV. Triphthongs.

aiə.

§ 78.

Oldham *aiə* mostly corresponds to:

a) Fr. *i* + Vowel (§ 25, B, b) *laiən* lion.
    Note: The above *is* also found with *əiə*.
b) OE. *ī* + *r* (§ 26) *šaiər* shire.
c) Fr. *i* + *r* (§ 26) *skwaiər* squire.

2. ME. *ē* before *r*.

    (§ 19, 2, 2) *kwaiər* quire.
    (§ 19, 2, 3) *kwaiər* choir.
    (§ 19, 2, 4, a) *fraiər* friar.
    (§ 19, 2, 5, b) *inkwaiər* enquire.

ęuə.

§ 79.

Oldham *ęuə* corresponds to ME. *ū* before *r*.

1. ME. *ū* + *r* (§ 32).
   a) OE. *ū bęuə^r* bower, *šęuə^r* shower.
   b) Sc. *ū kęuə^r* sit down.
   c) Fr. *ou flęuə^r* flour.
   d) Fr. *oë pęuə^r* power.

oïə (very rare).

§ 80.

Oldham *oïə* corresponds to:

1. ME. *oi* + Vowel (§ 44, A, 2, a).
   a) Fr. *oi roiəl* royal.

əïə.

§ 81.

Oldham *əïə* corresponds mostly to ME. *ī* before *r*.

1. ME. *ī* + *r* (§ 26).
   a) OE. *ī əiə^rn* iron, *wəiə^r* wire.
   b) OE. *ȳ fəiə^r* fire, *məiə^r* mire.
   c) Fr. *i Empəiə^r* Empire (Theatre).

CHAPTER III

THE VOWELS IN UNACCENTED SYLLABLE$

SHORT VOWELS.

a.

§ 82.

ME. unaccented *a* shows two developments: 1. it becomes ǝ, 2. it disappears.

1. *a* > ǝ.

a) In unaccented initial syllables followed by the principal accent.

ME.	OD.	NE.
aboute	ǝbẹut	about
abufen	ǝbūn	above
afæred	ǝfiǝ*r*t	afraid
agate	ǝgẹ̄t	in action
agein	ǝgen, ǝgin	against
agréer	ǝgrī	agree.

b) In syllables preceded by the principal accent.

Christ(es)-masse	kǝ*r*smǝs krismǝs kesmǝs }	Christmas
bastard	bastǝ*r*t	bastard
busard	buzǝ*r*t	butterfly
couard	kẹuǝ*r*t	aoward

ME.	OD.	NE.
crustade (sk)	kustǝ*r*t	custard
mustard	mustǝ*r*t	mustarc

2. a) Unaccented ME. *a* so times disappears initiall

amende	*mend*	mend
aprentice	*prentis*	apprent
L. ad + lot + ment	*lotmǝnts*	allotme

b) Unaccented ME. *a* di pears between certain co nants.

cristal	*kristl*	crystal
hospital	*ǭ*r*spitl*	hospital
metal	*metl*	metal
principal	*prinsipl*	principǝ

c) Unaccented *a* disappears ween accented and secon syllables.

cumpanie	*kumpni*	compan
	seprǝt	separat

e.

ME. *e* has become *ǝ* or *i*, under certain circumstances it has also disappeared.

1. ME. *e* > *ǝ* or *i*.

a) Initially.

ME.	OD.	NE.
elevene	*ǝlevn* (*ilǝvn*)	eleven
escāpe	*eskēp* (*iskēp*)	escape
L. eventus	*ivent*	event.

b) In initial syllables followed by the principal accent.

deceit	*disēt*	deceit
deceive	*dise'v*	deceive
delit	*dilǝit*	delight.

c) In syllables preceded by the principal accent.

countesse	*kɛuntǝs*	countes
hundred	*undǝᵣt*	hundred
saclǣs	*suklǝs*	silly.

also in all plurals in *es* (= OD. *iz*).

herses	*ǝᵣsiz*	hearses
houses	*ɛuziz*	houses
macches	*matšiz*	matches.

d) In unaccented syllables, between the principal and the secondary accent, ME. unaccented *e* either becomes *ǝ* or disappears.

ME.	OD.	NE.
beverage	*bev(ǝ)ᵣidž* (*bebridž*)	beverage
draperie	*drap(ǝ)ri*	drapery
gadering	*gaɖ(ǝ)rin*	gathering
miserie	*miz(ǝ)ri*	misery
quērēle + ing	*kwar(ǝ)lin*	quarrelling.

2. ME. *e* in unaccented syllables disappears.

a) Between certain consonants (*dl, tl, pl, vl, bl, (kl, tl,) sl*).

castel	*kasl*	castle
ketel	*ketl*	kettle
level	*levl*	level
litel	*litl*	little
purpre	*pǝᵣpl*	purple
rẽdles	*ridl*	riddle
stuble	*stubl*	stubble.

b) Final unaccented *e* in all ME. words is dropped.

mīle	*mǝil*	mile
swēte	*swīt*	sweet.

c) In unaccented syllables between the principal and the secondary accent (cp. I, d).

i.

ME. *i* either remains as *i* in unaccented syllables or is dropped.

1. a) ME. *i* (*y*) remains finally.

ME.	OD.	NE.
em(p)ti	*emti*	empty
half-peni	*ǫpni*	half-penny
mani	*moni*	many
sely	*sili*	silly.

b) ME. *i* remains in final unaccented syllables when preceded by the principal accent.

coming	*kumin*	coming
finisshe	*finiš*	finish
punische	*puniš*	punish

ME.	OD.	NE.
radishe	*radiš*	radish
schilling	*šilin*	shilling

c) ME. *i* remains in initial lables followed by the ⌐cipal accent.

distreine	*distrẹ̄n*	distrain
distresse	*distres*	distress
disturbe	*dista⸢b*	disturb.

2. ME. *i* is dropped betw principal and secondary acce⸢

peni-wurthe	*penəþ*	penny-worth.

o.

ME. *o* in unaccented syllables is 1. retained or 2. > *ə*, or 3. disappears.

1. ME. *o* is retained initially, though it sometimes > *ə*.

ME.	OD.	NE.
obeien	*obẹ̄ⁱ* (*əbẹ̄ⁱ*)	obey
observe	*obsā⸢v* (*əbsā⸢v*)	observe
opinioun	*opīnjən* (*əpīnjən*)	opinion

2. ME. *o* > *ə* in final syl les after the principal accent.

ME.	OD.	NE.
bulloke	*bulək*	bullock
confort	*kumfət*	comfort
galopen	*galəp*	gallop
sirope	*serəp*	syrup.

3. ME. *o* disappears betw principal and secondary syll (rare).

nǭ + ⎱bodi	*nǭbri*	nobody
sum + ⎰	*sụmbri*	somebo⸢

u (ü).

ME. *u* (*ü*) in unaccented syllables becomes *ə*, or dissappears

ME.	OD.	NE.
naturel	*nat(ə)rel*	natural.

LONG VOWELS.

$\bar{a}$.

§ 83.

MF. $\check{a}$ in unaccented syllables becomes ϑ, or i.

1. ME. $\bar{a} > \vartheta$.

ME.	OD.	NE.
conestāble	*konstəbl*	constable
speciāl	*spēšəl*	special.

2. ME. $\bar{a} > i$ before $d\check{z}$.

ME.	OD.	NE.
langāge	*laŋgwidž*	language
sauvāge	*savidž*	savage.

$\ddddot{\varrho}$.

ME. $\ddddot{\varrho}$ in unaccented syllables has become ϑ or i.

1. ME. $\ddddot{\varrho} > \vartheta$.

ME.	OD.	NE.
harneis (harnẹs)	*a^{r}nəs*	harness

ME.	OD.	NE.
paleis (palẹs)	*paləs*	palace.

2. ME. $\ddddot{\varrho} > i$.

ME.	OD.	NE.
cruẹl	*krẹuil*	cruel.

$\bar{\varrho}$.

ME. $\bar{\varrho}$ in unaccented syllables has become either ϑ or i, or has disappeared.

1. ME. $\bar{\varrho} > \vartheta$ in final syllables.

ME.	OD.	NE.
banẹre	*banə^r*	banner
bouchẹr	*butšə^r*	butcher
rivẹr	*rivə^r*	river.

2. ME. $\bar{\varrho} > i$ in final syllables.

ME.	OD.	NE.
beautẹ	*bjūti*	beauty
crüeltẹ	*krẹuilti*	cruelty
plentẹ	*plenti*	plenty.

3. ME. $\bar{\varrho}$ has disappeared between certain letters (*tl*, *dl*).

ME.	OD.	NE.
catẹl	*katl*	cattle
caudẹl	*kǭdl*	caudle.

Ī.

ME. ī in unaccented syllables became ə or i, or disappeared.

1. ME. ī > ə.

ME.	OD.	NE.
velīm	veləm*	vellum
venim	venəm*	venom.

* These are rare words in the dialect.

2. ME. ī > i.

ME.	OD.	NE.
compaignīe	kumpni	compaı
musīke	mjūsik	music
promīsen	promis	promisı

3. ME. ī disappears betv certain letters (sn, tn).

ME.	OD.	NE.
bāsīn	bēsn	basin
curtīn	kə˞tn	curtain
	(kə˞tnə˞)	
reisīn	rēzn	raisin.

Ō.

ME. ǭ becomes either ə or o, or disappears in unaccented syllables.

1. ME. ǭ > ə in final unaccented syllables.

ME.	OD.	NE.
(tresǭr)	tresə˞	treasure.

2. ME. ǭ > o when it a secondary accent.

ME.	OD.	NE.
catalǭge	katəlog	catalogı
dialǭge	dəialog	dialoguı

3. ME. ǭ > ə, or disapp between the principal and secondary accents.

ME.	OD.	NE.
histǭrie	ist(ə)ri	history
memǭrie	mem(ə)ri	memorʲ
victǭrie	vikt(ə)ri	victory.

Ū.

ME. ū becomes ə or disappears.

1. ME. ū > ə in unaccented final syllables.

ME.	OD.	NE.
colour	kulə˞	colour
favour	favə˞	favour

ME.	OD.	NE.
jelous	dželəs	jealous
labour	labə˞	labour.

2. ME. ū disappears betw principal and secondary acceı

ME.	OD.	NE.
particūlēr	pə˞tikelə˞	particul
regūlēr	reglə˞	regular.

ǖ.

ME. ǖ > ə, i or u.

1. ǖ > ə in unaccented syllables in.

ME.	OD.	NE.
mesǖre	mezə^r	measure
natü̆re	nētə^r	nature
	(nētd̄ə^r)	
pastǖre	pastə^r	pasture.

2. ǖ > i in unaccented syllables in:

ME.	OD.	NE.
minǖte	minit	minute.

3. ǖ > ju in secondary syllables in:

avenǖe	avenju	avenue
valǖe	valju	value
vertǖ	və^rtju	virtue.

DIPHTHONGS.

ai, ei.

§ 84.

ME. *ai, ei* in unaccented syllables has become ə or *i* or has disappeared.

1. *ai, ei* > ə.

ME.	OD.	NE.
conseil	keunsəl	counsel
	(keuńsil)	
duzain	duz(ə)n	dozen
Romain	Rōmən	Roman
travaille	trav(ə)l	travel.

Note: Some of the above also appear with *i* or drop the diphthong.

2. *ai, ei* > *i.*

ME.	OD.	NE.
chimnée	tšimbli	chimney
foreine	furin	foreign
fountaine	feuntin	fountain
touail	teuil	towel.

3. ME. *ai, ei* disappears between certain consonants.

bataile	batl	battle
botel	botl (bokl)	bottle
certain	sə̄^rtn	certain
	(sǟ^rtin)	
sodein	sudn	sudden
vitaille	witlz	victuals.

au.

ME. *au* in unaccented syllables becomes ə.

ME.	OD.	NE.
almaunde	ǭmənd	almond
ǧiaunt	džəiənt	giant
marchaunt	mā^rtš(ə)nt*	merchant
servaunt	sǟ^rv(ə)nt	servant.

* Note: In certain combinations this ə almost disappears.

A notable exception to the above rule is

ME.	OD.	NE.
orenǧe	orindž̆	orange.

$ęu, ęu.$

ME. $ęu, ęu$ in unaccented syllables remains as ju or u.

ME.	OD.	NE.
corfeu	$kə̄rfju$	curfew
neveu	$nevju$	nephew
Hebręu	$ībru$	Hebrew.

$oi, ǫu, ǫu$

do not occur in unaccented syllables, except in some cases of w
sentence stress.

B. Weak Syllables.

§ 85.

1. The ME. syllable *we* (NE. = *ow*) has become weakened to $ə$ in the OD.

ME.	OD.	NE.
arwe	$arə$	arrow
barwe	$barə$	barrow
schadwe	$šadə$	shadow
swalowe	$swalə$	swallow(vb)
wilwe	$wilə$	willow.

2. The ME. final syllable-*ward* becomes -$ərd$, -$ərt$ in the OD.

awkward	$ǫkərt$	awkward
bak-warde	$bakert$	backward
forward	$forərd$	forward.

Note: The ME. word *toward* (OE. *tóweard*) has become contracted to $tǭrd$ (= NE. *toward*).

3. A similar contraction taken place with the final syl les -*worth* and -*what* in c pounds. They appear as $əþ$ $ət$ respectively.

ME.	OD.	NE.
peni-wurthe	$penəþ$	penny-worth
sumwhat	$sumət$	somewh

4. Initial syllables followe the principal accent have been in (cp. also a in unstressed lables § 82):

bicause	koz	because
delivren	$livər$	deliver
entisen	$təis$	entice
ENE. ta-bacco	$bakə$	tobacco.

For examples of weak Sentence Stress cp. Inflexion — Auxil Verbs and Pronouns.

CHAPTER IV

THE CONSONANTS.

I. LABIALS.

p.

§ 86.

I. Initially *p* has been preserved.

ME.	OD.	NE.
path	*paþ*	path
peni	*peni*	penny
plaie, pleie	*plẹ̄ⁱ*	play
pot	*pot*	pot
pound	*pẹund, pund*	pound
proud	*prẹud*	proud
pẹ̄s	*pẹ̄s*	peace
puddiug	*pudn*	pudding
püre	*pjüəʳ*	pure
put	*put, pət*	put.

II. Medially.

ME.	OD.	NE.
spẹ̄ke	*spẹ̄k*	speak
sparwe	*sparə*	sparrow
sperit	*sperit*	spirit
appel	*apə, ap-pə*	apple
chaumpioun	*tšompjən*	champion
gospel	*gospəl*	gospel
pāper	*pɑpəʳ*	paper
whispere	*wispəʳ*	whisper
April(l)e	*April*	April
poplēr	*popləʳ*	poplar
purpre	*pəʳpl*	purple

ME.	OD.	NE.
Septembre	*Septembəʳ*	September
simple	*simpəl*	simple
upwarde	*upəʳdə*	upwards.

p is dropped:

α) Before *b.*

cupborde	*kubəʳt*	cupboard
rasp + berie	*razbri*	raspberry.

β) In the combination *mpt.*

empti (emti)	*emti*	empty
tempt	*temt*	tempt.

ME. *p* has become *b* in the following:[1]

baptisen	*babtəiz*	baptize
lopster	*lobstəʳ*	lobster
pibbel-stọn	*pebl*	pebble.
(OE. papel-stān?)		

III. Finally *p* always retained.

1. In ME. final position.

chẹ̄p	*tšīp, tšīəp*	cheap
dẹ̄p	*dīp, dīəp*	deep
hẹ̄p	*hīp, hīəp*	heap

---

[1] Cp. Bradley, M. L. Q. I, 27.

6*

ME.	OD.	NE.
hemp	*hemp*	hemp
scharp	*šaᵣp*	sharp.

2. In NE. final position.

cuppe	*kup*	cup
helpe	*elp*	help

ME.	OD.	NE.
laumpe	*lǭmp*	lamp
schāpe	*šēp*	shape
steppe	*step*	step
waspe	*wasp*	wasp.

b.

§ 87.

I. Initially *b* has remained.

ME.	OD.	NE.
bath	*baþ*	bath
bataile	*batl*	battle
bēre	*bēəᵣ, bīəᵣ*	bear
bēst	*bīəs(t)*	beast
blōd	*blud*	blood
bodi	*bodi*	body
boile	*bəil*	boil
bōk	*būk*	book
bute	*but*	but.

II. Medially.

abit	*abit*	habit
aboute	*əbȩut*	about
elbowe	*elbo*	elbow
husbonde	*usbənd*	husband
labour	*labəᵣ* *	labour
thim(b)el	*þimbl* **	thimble
timber	*timbəᵣ*	timber.

* Note 1. The ordinary word in the Dialect is *wark*.

** Note 2. *b* has been inserted after *m* and before *el* in:

nimel	*nimbl*	nimble
thimel	*þimbl*	thimble

ME.	OD.	NE.
February	*Febriwēᵣri*	Februa
humble	*umbl*	humble
tremblen	*trembl*	tremble
tumble	*tumbl*	tumble.

III. Finally.

In NE. final position *b* is retained, except after *m*.

α) Retained:

clubbe	*klub*	club
crabbe	*krab*	crab
gabbe	*gab*	gab
herbe	*jāᵣb*	herb
knobbe	*nob*	knob
ribbe	*rib*	rib.

β) Dropped:

cǫmb	*kǫm*	comb
dumb, domb	*dom, dum*	dumb
lamb, lomb	*lom*	lamb
clīmbe	*kləim*	climb
thombe, thumbe	*þum*	thumb.

Note: Final *b* is hardene *p* in

gossib	*gosip*	gossip.

f.

§ 88.

I. α) Initially *f* is usually retained.

ME.	OD.	NE.
fāder	*fēᵢdər*	father
fīnde	*fəind*	find
flesch	*flaiš, fleiš*	flesh, meat
flīe	*fləi*	fly
fōt	*fūt*	foot
foreine	*furin*	foreign.

β) Initial *f* has become *v* (an importation from the literary language, originally dialect of Kent):

fāne (Kent.	*vēᵢn**	vane
vāne)		
fat (Kent.	*vat*	vat
vat)		
fixen (Kent.	*vixn*	vixen.
vixen)		

* Note: "*wedər-kok*" is more common in the OD.

II. Medially.

biforen	*əfūər*	before
cofin	*kofin*	coffin
confort	*kumfər't*	comfort
defenden	*difend*	defend
defien	*difəi*	defy
griffoun	*grifin*	griffin
craft	*kraft*	craft
daft	*daft*	foolish
fifte	*fift*	fifth

ME.	OD.	NE.
gillofer	*džilifḷeuə'*	gillyflower
offre	*ofə'*	offer.

III. Finally.

α) In final position *f* mostly retained.

bēf	*bīf*	beef
chaufe	*tšēf*	chafe
delf	*delf*	a stone quarry
doffe	*dof*	doff
līf	*ləif*	life
scherefe	*šerif*	sheriff
strīf	*strəif*	strife
thēf	*þīf*	thief
wīf	*wəif*	wife.

β) In a few ME. words, the *f* has been dropped.

bailif, baili	*bēli*	bailiff
houswīf	*uzi*	huzzy
jolīf	*džoli*	jolly.

γ) *f* > *v* in the following.

calf	*kǫv*	calf
fīf	*faiv*	five
twelf	*twelv*	twelve
half	*ǫv*	half
of	*ov*	of.

Note: *f* in *half* is dropped in *ǫpni*-half-penny. — The OD. forms are derived from ME. inflected forms, *ov* is unstressed.

V.

§ 89.

ME. *v* = OD. *v* in all positions.

I. Initially.

ME.	OD.	NE.
verrei,verrai	*veri*	very
vertu	*vā^rtju*	virtue
vers	*vā^rs, ves*	verse
vois	*vois*	voice
viage	*vauədž* (*au!*)	voyage.

Note: Initial *v* > *f* in:

vecche	*fitš*	vetch.

II. a) Medially.

fever	*fēvə^r*	fever
hęven	*evn*	heaven
livre	*livə^r*	liver
rivēr	*rivə^r*	river
seven	*sevn*	seven
wives	*waivz*	wives.

b) Medial *v* has been dropped in:

dēvel	*dīl, dīəl*	devil

ME.	OD.	NE.
eveninge	*īn*	evening
ever	*ə̄^r*	ever
given	*gin*	given
ǫven	*ūn*	oven
over	*ǭə^r*	over
po(v)re	*pūə^r*	poor.

III. a) Finally (NE. position).

douve	*duv*	dove
drīve	*drəiv*	drive
glōve	*dluv*	glove
love	*luv*	love
schouve	*šuv*	shove.

b) Medial *v* > *f* in a cer number of words.

belēve	*bilīf*	belief

For explanation cp. Kö
Archiv CVI, 37.

W.

§ 90.

I. Initially.

α) ME. *w* has remained.

ME.	OD.	NE.
waǧe	*wēⁱdžəz*	wages
waite	*węt*	wait
waraunt	*warənt*	warrant
was	*woz*	was
wāter	*wētə^r, wēþə^r,wītə^r*	water
wēke	*wīk*	week
werre	*wā^r*	war

ME.	OD.	NE.
wīn	*wəin*	wine
wisshe	*wīš*	wish
wode	*wud*	wood
wolde, wulde	*wud*	would
word	*wə̄^rd*	word.

β) Initial *w* dropped befor

wrappen	*rap*	wrap
wrechen	*ratš*	to stre

ME.	OD.	NE.
wrestlen	*rasl, rosl*	wrestle
wringe	*riŋg*	wring
wrīte	*rəit*	write
wrīthe	*rəiđ*	writhe
wriþən	*riđn*	twisted.

Note: An initial *w* has been prefixed before ME. *ǭ* cp. § 27, III.

II. Medially.

a) Consonant + *w*. — The groups *dw, sw, tw*

α) preserve the *w* in the OD. except, β) before velar vowels and in unaccented syllables.

α)

dwellen	*dwel*	dwell
dwarf,	*dwaᵣf*	dwarf
dwerf		
dwindle	*dwindle*	dwindle
swap	*swap*	a stroke
swelten	*swelty*	sultry
swēte	*swīt*	sweet
swōte	*swot*	to sweat
twine	*twɔin*	twine
twinklen	*twiŋkl*	twinkle
twist	*twist*	twist.

β)

1. Before Velar Vowels.

hwō > hō	*ū*	who
hwōm > hōm	*ūm*	whom
hwās > hōs	*ūz*	whose
swa	*sǭ, sǭ, so*	so
swērd	*sǭᵣd*	sword
twǭ	*tṵ̄*	two
þwong	*þoŋ*	thong.

2. In unaccented Syllables.

ME.	OD.	NE.
swich, swuch	*sitš, sutš*	such.

b) Before Vowels.

1. Dropped before velar Vowels and in unaccented syllables.

α) Before Velar Vowels.

(al)swa	*(ǭ)lsǭ*	(al)so.

β) In unaccented syllables.

alway	*ǭləz*	always
answare	*ǫnsəʳ*	answer
bacward	*bakəʳdz*	backwards
bōtswain	*bǭsn*	boatswain
foreward	*forəd*	forward
grundes-wilie	*grunsl*	groundsel
houswīf	*uzi*	housewife
peni-wurth	*penəþ*	penny-worth.

2. *w* has been inserted before *a* vowel in:[1]

langage	*languidž*	language.

III. Finally *w* has always dropped in NE. final position being weakened to *ə*. This is due to the unaccented position.

arwe	*arə*	arrow
barwe	*barə*	barrow
medwe	*medə*	meadow
schadwe	*šadə*	shadow
widwe	*widə*	widow
wilwe	*wilə*	willow
ȝelwe	*jalə*	yellow.

Note: ME. *felawe*, however, appears mostly as *feli*,

---

[1] Cp. Köppel "Spelling Pronunciations" p. 23,

hw (wh).

§ 83.

ME. *hw* (*wh*) has either disappeared totally (cp. p. 87, a, β) or become *w*. It only occurs initially.

hw > *w*.

ME.	OD.	NE.
what	*wot*	what

ME.	OD.	NE.
when	*wen*	when
whēr(e)	*wīər* (*wə̄ʳ*)	where
which	*wits̆*	which
whistle	*wisl*	whistle
whīt	*wait*	white.
	(*wəit*)	

m.

§ 84.

ME. *m* has always remained.

I. Initially.

ME.	OD.	NE.
man, moᴅ	*mon*	man
mete	*mēt*	meat
miche, moche	*mits̆*	much
mīn, mi	*məi*	my
mōder	*mudəʳ*	mother
mountaine	*meuntin*	mountain
month	*meuþ*	month
myghte	*məit*	might.

II. Medially.

smellen	*smel*	smell (vb)
smoᵭren	*smūəʳ*	to suffocate
almesse	*ōməs*	alms
amounten	*əmeunt*	amount
damage	*damidz̆* (*domidz̆*)	damage
hamer	*oməʳ*	hammer
ʒemer (sad)	*joməʳ*, *jaməʳ*	to grieve.

ME.	OD.	NE.
companie	*kumpni*	compaᴅ
humble	*umbl*	humble
laumpe	*lomp*	lamp
noumpēre	*umpəiəʳ*	umpire
simple	*simpl*	simple
þombe	*þum*	thumb.

Note: ME. *m* > *n* befo in the following.

am(e)te	*ant*	ant.

III. Finally.

bosum	*buzm*	bosom
dreem	*drīəm*, *drem*	dream
ham	*wum*	home
ram	*rom*	ram
roum	*reum*	room
come	*kum*	come
nāme	*nēⁱm*	name
swimme	*swim*	swim
tīme	*təim*	time.

II. DENTALS.

t.

§ 85.

ME. *t* has remained in all positions.

I. Initially.

ME.	OD.	NE.
tāle	*tēⁱl*	tale
tīme	*təim*	time
toun	*tęun*	town
tour	*tęuəʳ*	tower
tunge	*tuŋg*	tongue.

II. Medially.

steir	*stīəʳ, stəʳ*	stair
straw	*strēⁱ*	straw
bataile	*batl*	battle
curtin	*kəʳtnəʳ*	curtain
fitlock, fetlack	*fetlock*	fetlock
pertriche	*pāʳtridž*	partridge.

In many words where *t* occurs before *r* (*ər*), it becomes *tđ* or *þ*. This rule is not so invariable however as in the neighbouring dialects (cp. Hargreaves § 74, 2).

beter	*betđəʳ* (*betəʳ*)	better
creature	*krēþəʳ* (*krētəʳ*)	creature
cutten + leg	*kutđəʳ- leg* (*kutəʳ- leg*)	a hoop of a barrel used as a hoop to play with
Ęster	*Āsþəʳ, Ēsþəʳ*	Easter

ME.	OD.	NE.
maister	*mesþəʳ* (*mestəʳ*)	master
matere	*matþəʳ*	matter
wāter	*wēþəʳ* (*wētəʳ*)	water
winter	*winþəʳ*	winter.

t has been dropped medially between *s*, *f* and *l*, *m*, *n*.

Christes- masse	*krismes*	Christmas
listene	*lisn*	listen
often	*ofn*	often
soften	*sofn*	soften
thrǫstel	*þrosl*	throstle
whistle	*wisl*	whistle.

Note: *t* > *r*:

Span. patata *porita*   potato.

Contrary to some neighbouring dialects *t* before ME. *ü* does not become *tš* but remains as *t* (cp. Hargreaves § 74, 8 and Horn, Unters. p. 86 ff.)

fournitüre	*fornitəʳ*	furniture
fortüne	*fortin*	fortune
natüre	*nętəʳ* (*netđəʳ*)	nature
pastüre	*pastəʳ* (*pasđəʳ*)	pasture.

III. Finally (in ME. and NE. final positions).

at	*at*	at
aught	*ǭt*	aught
aunt(e)	*ǭnt, ęnt*	aunt

ME.	OD.	NE.
bǫt	bǫt	boat
holt	baut	bolt
bat	at	hat
areste	ərest	arrest
bǫte	būt	boot
berste	brasl	burst
chiste	tšist, kist	chest
faute	faul	fault
fighte	fəit	fight.

Final (ME. and NE.) *t* has been assimilated to preceding *s*.

beste	bīəst (pl. beast bīəs)	
cruste	krus﹇pl. / krəs﹛kru-sisez	crust
ğiste	džois (pl. joist dsoisiz)	
leste	les	leat
nest	niz (pl. nest. niziz) (nīst)	

Final *t* has been dropped before a word beginning with a consonant.

būte	bə', bo', bai' but	
lŏte	le	let
put	po	put

ME.	OD.	NE.
Cp. Whit-sundei	Wisn(di)	Whitsu day.

Note: In some of the al words *t* often becomes *r* (als ME. *gete*), that is to say when stand before a vowel.

lete	ler	let
gete	ger	get
put	pər	put.

A final *t* has been ad (sometimes in LME.) to the f wing.

auncien(t)	ēnšənt	ancient
fēsaun(t)	fəznt	pheasan
tirann(t)	təirənt	tyrant
ǭnes	wunst, wənst	once
gisér	gizərt (gizə'n)	gizzard
hērce	hə̄'st	hearse
scurf	skruft	scruff
snevien	snift	sniff
tiffen	tift	good or

Note: The forms against whilst are not found in the lect. They are əgin and wəil w out *st* as in ME.

d.

§ 86.

I. Initially ME. *d* has remained in the OD.

ME.	OD.	NE.
day, dai	dēⁱ	day
dauncen	dǭns, dains, dons	dance

ME.	OD.	NE.
dar	dār, də̄ʳ	dare
dęl	dīəl	deal
dēẓe, dīe	dəi, (dī)	die
doughter	dautəʳ	daughte
dūble	dubl	doubl
dumb, domb	dom	dumb.

II. Medially.

1. ME. *d* has been preserved.

ME.	OD.	NE.
body, bodi	*bodi*	body
bridel	*brəidl*	bridle
cinder, sinder	*sindər*	cinder
gardin	*gārdn, gārdin*	garden
jaundis (jannis)	*jǭndis*	jaundice
medicine	*medsin*	medicine
kindle	*kindl*	kindle
kidnẹre	*kidni*	kidney
medle	*medl*	meddle.

2. Intervocalic *d* in unaccented syllables has become *r*.

ĕny, ani + bodi	*anibri*	anybody
nǭbodi	*nǭbri*	nobody
sum, som + bodi	*sụmbri*	somebody.

3. *d* after *n* has disappeared by assimilation medially in the combinations *nds, ndf, ndl, ndn.*

nds

answare	*ǭnsər, onsər*	answer
groundswell	*grụnsel*	groundsel

ndf

graund + fader	*gronfēidər*	grandfather
land } + lọrd lond }	*lonlọrt*	landlord

ndl

candel	*konl*	candle
trendelen	*trunl*	trundle
nēdle	*nīl*	needle

ndn

brandnewe	*bron-njū*	brandnew
haboun-dance	*abunəns*	abundance.

4. ME. *d* between Vowel and *r* > *đ.*

ME.	OD.	NE.
bladdre	*bleđər (bledər)*	bladder
(didder)	*diđər*	to tremble
fader	*fēiđər*	father
fodder	*fođər*	fodder
gadere	*gađər*	gather
laddre	*lađər (ladđər)*	ladder
mọder	*muđər*	mother
poudre	*peuđər (pẹuđər)*	powder
wẹder	*weđər*	weather.

ME. *d* after Consonant + *r* generally becomes *dđ; ddr > dđr,* and *dr > đr,* cp. *bleđər, bledər =* "bladder" and *lađər, ladđər =* "ladder" above.

	glenđər (glendər)	to stare
	linđər (lindər)	to tie up
wonder	*wunđər (wundər)*	wonder
hundred	*undđred, undred*	hundred
childre	*tšilđər*	children.

III. Finally.

ME. *d* has a) remained as *d* or b) become *t* under certain conditions or c) has disappeared.

a) 1. In ME. final position.

balled	*baud*	bald
bẹrd	*biərd*	beard
blọd	*blud*	blood
cōld	*kaud*	cold
glad	*dlad*	glad.

2. In NE. final position.

ME.	OD.	NE.
almaunde	ǫmənd	almond
cloude	tlęud	cloud
ende	end	end
knēde	nīəd, nīd	knead
ladde	lad	lad
ǫld	aud	old.

b) Final *d* > *t* 1. in the preterite and past participle of many verbs and 2. a large number of other words.

1.

axede	akst	asked
hōpede	ōpt	hoped
lokede	lūkt	looked
passede	past	passed
crabbe + ed	krabt	ill-tempered
crencled	kriŋklt	crinkled
dased	deⁱzt	dazed
favoured	favəᵣt	favoured
grisel + ed	grizlt	grizzled
hanged	aŋgt	hanged
ōpen + ed	opənt	opened
sēmede	semt	seemed
smorthered	smūᵣt	smothered
teried	tarit	tarried
blended	blendit	blended.

2.

afraried	afiəᵣt	afraid
awkward	ǫkəᵣt	awkward
bakward	bakəᵣt	backward
band	bant	band, string

ME.	OD.	NE.
behinde	behint (bihənt)	behind
beyonde	bijont	beyond
blīnd	blint	blind
chīld	tšəilt, tšilt	child
fēld	fīəlt, fīlt	field
fǫld	faud	fold
for(th)ward	forət (forəd)	forward
hand, hond	ont	hand
inwarde	inəᵣt	inward
londlǫrd	lonlǫᵣt	landlord
solide	solit	solid
thousand	þęusənt	thousand
toward	tuəᵣt(tǫᵣd)	toward •
wisard	wizəᵣt	wizard
wǫrd	wəᵣt	word.

For further examples with explanations cp. Horn "Gutturallaute" p. 38 ff.

c) *d* has disappeared after *n* in the following (see also above).

and	an	aud
bunden	bun	constipated
funden	fon, fun	found
grand	gron	grand
ground	grun	ground
wunden	wun	wound.

Note: *d* has not been inserted in:

boun	bęun	bound (adj.)
lēne	lan	lend.

th, (þ).

§ 87.

I. Initially *þ* has remained except in unaccented words and sometimes before *w*.

1. *þ* has remained.

ME.	OD.	NE.
thāwe	þǫ	thaw

ME.	OD.	NE.
thēf	þīf	thief
thorn	þǫᵣn	thorn
thumbe	þum	thumb
thunder	þunəᵣ	thunder.

2. Initial þ > ð in unaccented in unaccented words.

ME.	OD.	NE.
that	ðat	that
þę	ðī	thee
þei	ðē	they
their	ðēə^r (ðə^r)	their
thenne	ðen	then
thęre	ðīə^r, ðē^r	there
þīn	ðəi(n)	thy, thine
this	ðis	this
þou, þu	ðęu	thou
þōs	ðūəz	those.

Note: Used interrogatively, the 2nd pers sing. appears as tə e. g. es-tə = "hast thou"? wil-tə? wilt thou? This is a process of assimilation to the preceding t.

It even becomes t in such combinations as "Wotəst t'sēⁱ?" = What dost thou say?

II. Medially and Finally.

1. þ remained.

helthe + y	elþi	healthy

ME.	OD.	NE.
nōthing	nuþing, nuþiŋk	nothing
mouth	męuþ	mouth
path	paþ	path
tōth	tūþ	tooth
treuthe	treuþ	truth.

2. In the following unaccented word þ > ð.

with	wið	with.

3. thw > thw or w.

þwytel	þwitl, witlwhittle	
þwyten	þwəit	to cut
þwaken	þwak,wak	thwack.

Note 1: ME. þwong has lost it w before o:

þwong	þoŋg	thong.

Note 2: NE. thwart (< ON. þvert) is seldom found in the dialect. The same thing applies to the derivatives of this word.

th, (ð).

§ 88.

1. ME. þ (ð) has remained medially and in NE. final position.

ME.	OD.	NE.
brọther	brudə^r	brother
either	ēⁱðə^r	either
ferthing	fa^rðin	farthing ·
lather	loðə^r	lather
nouther	nǭðə^r	neither
bāthe	bēⁱð	bathe
bọthe	bụ̄ð	booth

ME.	OD.	NE.
bręthe	brīð	breath
smọthe	smūð	smooth.

Note 1: ð > þ however in:

bōthe	būəþ	both
benęthe	binīəþ	beneath.

Note 2: Concerning plural forms męuþs &c. cp. Accidence.

2. ME. *þ* (*đ*) = *d*.

ME.	OD.	NE.
aforthe	*əfōͬd*	afford
fīthel	*fidl*	fiddle
morđer	*mōͬdəͬ*	murder
	(*mōͬđəͬ*)	
spīther	*spəidəͬ*	spider
	(*spəiđəͬ*)	

ME.	OD.	NE.
swathele	*swadl*	swaddle.

Note: *kud* (could) > OE. *couþe* shows same analogical formation as in lit. Engl.

clǭthes	*tlūəz*	clothes.

S.

§ 89.

Initially.

ME. *s* has remained in simple and in compound words.

ME.	OD.	NE.
certain	*sāͬtin*	certain
sand	*sond*	sand
salt	*sǭt*	salt
spę̄ke	*spēͥk*	speak
stǭn	*stūən*	stone
handsom	*ansəm*	handsome
him-self	*issél, isél* *issén, isén*	himself
me-self	*mis(s)él* *mis(s)én*	myself
in-sīde	*insəid*	inside.

Finally.

1. ME. *s* has remained α) in words ending in *s*, and β) in the ending of the Nom. Pl. and the Gen. case, when an unvoiced consonant precedes.

1.

fāce, fūs	*fę̄s*	face
gę̄s	*gīs* [1]	geese
kiss	*kis* [1]	kiss
mous	*męus*	mouse
vois	*vois*	voice.

2.

ME.	OD	NE.
bōkes	*būks*	books
cates	*kats*	cats
schipes	*šips*	ships
wifes	*wəif's*	wife's
wulfes	*wulf's*	wolf's.

2. After Voiced Consonants or Vowels ME. final inflexional *s* appears as *z*.

bedes	*bedz*	beds
clǭthes	*tlūəz*	clothes
daies	*dēz*	days
(dōth) does	*duz*	does
fēldes	*fīlds*	fields
loves	*luvz*	loves
pens	*penz*	pens.

3. ME. *s* has been dropped where it has been mistaken for a plural ending.

chemise	*šimi*	chemise
chery (Fr. čerise)	*tšeri, tširi*	cherry
pę̄s	*pēͥ*	pea
rēdels	*ridl*	riddle.

---

[1] The common word in the dialect is *bəs* (*bus*).

4. *s* has been added during the ME. period (original plural forms).

ME.	OD.	NE.
belwe(s)	*baliz(iz)*	bellows
galwes	*galeziz*	braces
smal-pokke	*smǫpoks*	small-pox
trewes	*trẹus*	truce.

Note: ME. *s* = French *s*:

1. French voiceless *s* remains as *s*.

bāsin	*bẹsn*	basin
counseil	*kẹunsil*	counsel

ME.	OD.	NE.
hospitalle	*ǫ͞ʳspitl*	hospital
lossoun	*lesn*	lesson
sauce + age	*sosidž̆,* *sosindzəʳ*	sausage.

2. ME. *s* (= Fr. *s*) + *i* > *š*.

misiōn	*mišn*	mission
nacion, nacioun	*nẹšn*	nation
pacient	*pẹšnt*	patient
special	*spẹ̄ʳšl*	special
staciōn	*stẹ̄ʳšn*	station
sūcre, sügre	*šugəʳ*	sugar
(Lat. assūmere)	*əšūm*	assume.

z.

§ 90.

ME. *z* occurs medially and finally.

I. Medially ME. *z* remains unchanged.

ME.	OD.	NE.
besom	*bīzm*	besom
frosen	*frozn*	frozen
husbonde(?)	*uzbənt*	husband
fẹsaun	*feznt*	pheasant
prisoun	*prizn*	prison.

II. ME. *z* has remained in NE. final position.

(as)sise	*səiz*	size
chẹse	*tšīz*	cheese
ẹse + y	*jezi*	easy
plẹse	*plez*	please
wīse	*wəiz*	wise.

Note: ME. *z* = French *z*:

ME. *z* (= Fr. *z*) remains as *z*.

ME.	OD.	NE.
excūsen	*ekskjūz*	excuse
mẹsüre	*mezəʳ*	measure
plẹsüre	*plezəʳ*	pleasure
preisen	*prez*	praise
refüsen	*rifjūz*	refuse
üsen	*jūz*	use.

The form *trezəʳ* for "treasure" is however not noted in any glossary of the OD., tho' it occurs in East Lincoln., cp. Wright EDD.

Note: *siđəʳz* (scissors) with *đ* for *z*, cp. Horn, Anglia-Beiblatt XVII, 64, and Ritter, Archiv CXV, 175.

š.

§ 91.

I. Initially ME. *š* has remained.

ME.	OD.	NE.
schadwe	*šadə*	shadow
schip	*šip*	ship
schutte	*šut*	shut
schort	*šǭʳt*	short.

II. Medially ME. *š* has also remained.

bisshop	*bišəp*	bishop
buschel	*bušl*	bushel
cuishin	*kwīšin*	cushion
musheroun	*mušrǫum*	mushroom.

III. Finally.

1. ME. *š* has remained in α) ME. and β) NE. final positions.

α)

busch	*buš (buiš)*	bush

ME.	OD.	NE.
disch	*dīš*	dish
fisch	*fiš*	fish
flesch	*flēiš*	flesh.

β)

dasshe	*daiš*	dash
lasshe	*laiš*	lash
wasshe	*wē'š, weš*	wash
wisshe	*wiš*	wish.

2. In place of ME. *sch* we find *s* in:

asche	*es*	ash.

Note: ME. *sk* > *s* in:

menske-ful	*mensfu*	decent, neat.

Cp. Horn "Gutturallaute" p. 19 ff.

tš.

§ 92.

I. Initially.

ME. *ch* remains as *tš*.

ME.	OD.	NE.
chaine	*tšiən*	chain
chalk	*tšǭk*	chalk
chaunce	*tšons*	chance
chaunge	*tšondž*	change
chap (-man)	*tšap*	chap.

II. Medially.

1. ME. *ch* remains except in certain combinations.

boucher	*butšəʳ*	butcher
kicchen	*kitšən*	kitchen
marchaunt	*mārtsənt*	merchant.

2. ME. *lch (ltš)*, *nch (ntš)* have either remained as *ltš*, *ntš* or have become *lš*, *tš* as in lit. English

ME.	OD.	NE.
belke (belche)	*bel(t)š*	belch
bench	*ben(t)š*	bench
braunche	*brǭn(t)š* *bron(t)š*	branch
inche	*in(t)š*	inch
wenche	*wen(t)š*	wench.

* Note: Medially the combination *ltš*, *ntš* appears as *ltš*, *ntš* finally as *lš*, *nš*.

III. Finally.

1. ME. *tš* remains in accented syllables (NE. final position).

ME.	OD.	NE.
bicche	*bitš*	bitch
blęche	*blęⁱtš*	bleach
focche	*fotš*	fetch
pręche	*prętš*	preach
sēche	*sītš*	seek.

Note: Observe *k* in *flik (flitš) = flitch.*

2. ME. *ch* in unstressed syllables appears both as α) *dž* and β) *tš*.

α)

ME.	OD.	NE.
cartidge	*kaʳtridž*	cartridge
knowlęche	*nolidž*	knowledge

β)

ME.	OD.	NE.
cabbache	*kabitš*	cabbage
Northwiche	*Nōrþwitš*	Northwich
ostriche	*ostritš*	ostrich.

dž.

§ 93.

ME. *dž* appears in all positions, though it is occasionally pronounced *ž* in the combination *ndž*.

1. ME. *dž (ǧǵ)* = OE. *čǵ*.

ME.	OD.	NE.
brigge	*bridž*	bridge
egge	*edž*	edge
flegge	*fledž*	fledge
hegge	*edž*	hedge
migge	*midž*	midge
rigge	*ridž*	ridge
segge	*sedž*	sedge
wegge	*wedž*	wedge.

Note: Observe the two forms *Magi* and *Madž (= Maggie* and *Madge)* side by side as contractions for *Margeret.*

2. ME. *dž (j, g)* = Fr. *g, j.*

ME.	OD.	NE.
gail	*džēⁱl*	jail
general	*dženǝrǝl*	general
joine	*džǝin*	join
jüge	*džudž*	judge
engin	*indžin*	engine
religioun	*rilidžǝn*	religion.

3. *dž* in the Combination *ndž.*

daunger	*dǭn(d)žeʳ*	danger
henge	*in(d)ž*	hinge
orenge	*orin(d)ž*	orange
straunge	*strǭn(d)ž*	strange
straunger	*strǭn(d)zǝʳ*	stranger.

Note: The combination *ndž* is pronounced indifferently as *ndž* or *nž*, tho' the former is the more usual pronunciation when it stands medially.

n.

§ 94.

I. Initially *n* remains.

ME.	OD.	NE.
name	*nēⁱm*	name
nędle	*nīdl*	needle
night	*nīt*	night
noise	*noiz*	noise
now	*nęu*	now.

7

Note: *n* has, however, been dropped initially in the following words, it being falsely thought to belong to the indefinite article.

ME.	OD.	NE.
nadder, adder	*atəʳ*	poison
napron	*apəʳn*	apron
noumpēre	*ụmpəieʳ*	umpire.

II. Medially.

knē	*nī*	knee
knǭwe	*nǭ*	know
gnar	*nārlt*	cross-tempered
snaw	*snǭ, snǭ*	snow
snoute	*snẹut*	snout
binēđe	*binīəþ*	beneath
enemi	*inimi*	enemy
honest	*onist*	honest
moni	*moni*	many
peniʒ	*peni*	penny
almande	*ǭmənd*	almond
bench	*bentš*	bench
counte	*kẹunt*	count
ground	*grẹund, grụn(d)*	ground
hunte(r)	*ụntəʳ (ụnþəʳ)*	hunter
mountaine	*mẹuntin*	mountain
round	*rẹund*	round
straunge	*strǭndz*	strange.

2. *n* has been dropped.

α) In the combination *ln*.

kilne	*kil*	kiln
milne	*mil*	mill.

β) In the combination *mn*.

autumpne	*ǭtəm*	autumn
columne	*koləm*	column
dam(p)ne	*dom*	damn
ymp(n)e	*im*	hymn.

Note: *n* has been inserted medially in:

ME.	OD.	NE.
messaǧer	*mesinděəʳ*	messenger
passaǧer	*pasinděəʳ*	passenger
sauce-age	*sosinděəʳ*	sausage.

Cp. Luick, Archiv CXIV, 76.

III. Finally.

1. In ME. final position.

α) In stressed syllables *n* is retained.

boun	*bẹun*	prepared, ready.
man, mon	*mon*	man
quẹn	*kwīn*	queen
wīn	*wəin*	wine.

β) In unstressed syllables or words *n* is dropped.*

in	*i*	in
an	*a*	an, a.

* In some cases the *n* is still retained by analogy with inflected forms, cp. Köppel, Archiv CIV.

brazen	*brazn*	brazen
īren	*əiəʳn*	iron
ǭpen	*opn*	open
ǭven	*ūn*	oven.

2. In NE. final position usually retained.

bitwẹne	*bitwīn*	between
canne	*kon*	can, may
chaine	*tšiən*	chain
droune	*drẹun*	drown
foreine	*furīn*	foreign
grēne	*grīn*	green.

1.

§ 95.

I. Initially. ME. *l* has remained unchanged in the OD.

ME.	OD.	NE.
lamb	*lam, lom*	lamb
larǧe	*lārdž*	large
lẹde	*līd*	lead
level	*levl*	level
litel	*litl*	little
long	*loŋg*	long
lǫrd	*lǫrd*	lord
lond	*lond*	land
love	*luv*	love.

II. Medially.

a) Consonant + *l*.

blame	*blē͜ᶦm*	blame
blǫd	*blud*	blood
clẹne	*tlīn*	clean
clẹr	*tlīə͛*	clear
flesch	*flaᶦš, flēᶦš*	flesh, meat
flour	*flᵤə͛*	flour
flour	*flᵤə͛, flə͛*	flower
glad	*dlad*	glad
glǫrie	*dlǫri*	glory
place	*plẹs*	place
pleie	*plēᶦ*	play
slẹpe	*slīp*	sleep.

b) Before Vowels (and *w*).

colour	*kulə͛*	colour
delīt	*dilīt*	delight
Engeland	*Iŋglond*	England
felawe	*feli*	fellow
folwe	*folə(͛)*	follow
galwes	*galəsis*	braces
wilwe	*wilə(͛)*	willow.

c) Before Consonants.

ME. *l* has been dropped: α) before Labials, β) before Gutturals, γ) before Dentals.

α) Before Labials (*v, f, m*).

ME.	OD.	NE.
calf	*kǫv*	calf
half	*ǭf, ǭv (ēᶦf,*	half
	Rochdale)	
almannde	*ǭmənd*	almond
almes	*ǭmes, ǭmz*	alms
bal(s)me	*bǭm*	balm
calme	*kǭm*	calm.

β) Before Gutturals.

balke	*bǫk*	a log
folk	*fǫk (fok)*	folk
talken	*tǫk*	talk
walke	*wǭk*	walk
зolke	*jǫk*	yolk.

γ) Before Dentals.

alter	*ǭtə͛*	alter
bāld	*baud*	bold
balled	*bǭd*	bald
bolt	*bant*	bolt
cǭld	*kaud*	cold
colt	*kaut*	colt
fals	*fǫs*	sly, cunning
fǫlde	*faud*	fold (vb)
gǭld	*gaud*	gold
schulde*	*šud*	should
wolde,	*wud*	would.
wulde*		

* Note: Unaccented Words.

III. Finally.

1. In ME. final position: α) *l* has generally remained after palatal vowels, β) has disappeared after velar vowels.

α) Final *l* retained.

al	*ǭl (ǫ)*	all
crüél	*krüil*	cruel

7*

ME.	OD.	NE.
dẹ̄l	dīəl	deal
ful	ful (fū)	full
họ̄l	wul	whole.

β) Final *l* dropped.

al	ǭ (ǭl)	all
ball	bǭ	ball
cọ̄l	kū	cool
dọl	dau	dole
fọ̄l	fū	fool
foul	fẹu	foul
ful	fū (ful)	full
stol	stū	stool.

2. In NE. final position.

α) *l* has been retained.

ME.	OD.	NE.
ale	ẹ̄il	ale
falle	fǭl (fǭ)	fall
fille	fil	fill
mille	mil	mill
soule	saul	soul
stẹle	stẹ̄il	steal
tale	tẹ̄l	tale
telle	tel	tell.

β) *l* has been dropped.

calle	kǭ	call
falle	fǭ, fo (fǭl)	fall.

r.

§ 96.

I. Initially. ME. *r* has remained.

ME.	OD.	NE.
rain, rein	rẹ̄n	rain
rẹ̄de	rīd, rīəd	read
rẹ̄sonn	rẹ̄ən	reason
riche	ritš	rich
rīde	rəid	ride
ring	riŋg	ring
rivér	rivəʳ	river
rọ̄f	rūf	roof
rọ̄te	rūt	root
roum	rẹum	room
round	rẹund	round.

II. Medially.

a) Consonant + *r*.

braunche	brontš	branch
bringe	briŋg	bring
crẹpe	krīp, krīəp	creep
crūne	krẹun	crown
frẹ̄	frī	free
früt	früt	fruit

ME.	OD.	NE.
grẹ̄ne	grīn	green
prẹ̄st	prẹ̄st	priest
prīs	prais	price
schroud	šraud	shroud
sprẹde	sprīəd	spread
strẹte	strīt	street
strīf	straif	strife
trẹ̄	trī	tree
wrīte	rəit	write.

b) Before Vowels (and *w*) *r* is retained.

arwe	arə	arrow
berie	beri, bəri	berry
borwe	bore(ʳ)	borrow
carie	kari	carry
marie	mari	marry
Marie	Mẹ-ri (Mīəri)	Mary
mirie	məri (meri)	merry
sorwe	sorə(ʳ)	sorrow
to-morwe	tu-morə(ʳ)	to-morrow
verrai, verrei	veri, vəri	very.

c) Before Consonants.

α) ME. *r* has been much weakened, but mostly retained, cp. § 2, "*r*".

ME.	OD.	NE.
arm	*ā͜rm*	arm
art, ert	*ā͜rt, ə͜rt*	art
cōrn	*kə͜rn*	corn
hard	*ā͜rd*	hard
harpe	*ā͜rp*	harp
kerve	*kā͜rv, kə͜rv*	carve
lērne	*lā͜rn*	learn
marbre, marble	*mā͜rbl*	marble
purpre	*pə͜rpl*	purple
scharp	*šā͜rp*	sharp
schort	*šə͜rt*	short
sĕrve	*sā͜rv*	serve
word	*wə͜rd*	word
werk	*wā͜rk*	work (sb)
worth, wurth	*wə͜rþ*	worth.

β) But before *s*, *r* has been dropped.

berste	*bust (brast)*	burst
hors	*os*	horse
first	*fust, fost*	first
worse, wurse	*wus (wə͜r)*	worse
worsted	*wustid*	worsted.

Note: *uəs = hoarse* < ME. *hǫrs* or *hǫs* had originally no *r*, cp. Hargreaves § 66, 2, Note.

d) Metathesis of ME. medial *r*.

α) Metathesis has taken place in:

berste	*brast*	burst
berne	*brun, brən*	burn
grinne	*gə͜rn*	grin

ME.	OD.	NE.
kirnel	*krindl (kə͜rnel)*	kernel
scurf	*skruf*	scurf
hundred	*undə͜rt*	humdred.

β) Double forms are to be found in:

firmenty	*fə͜rmetri frəmetri*	frumenty
gredil	*gridl gərdl*	a bakestone.

Note: Contrary to the literary language, metathesis has not taken place in:

brid	*brid*	bird
crudde	*krud*	curd.

III. Finally.

In ME. and NE. Final Position *r* is retained in a strongly weakened form, cp. Note *.

fāder	*fādə͜r, fēidə͜r*	father
fīr	*fəier*	fire
modor	*muðə͜r*	mother
sür, seür	*šūə͜r*	sure
tour	*teuə͜r*	tower
bĕre	*bę̄ə͜r*	bear
care	*kę̄ə͜r*	care
childre	*tšildə͜r, tšildə͜r*	children
ēre	*īə͜r*	ear
hęre	*īə͜r*	here
mǭre	*mūə͜r*	more
oure	*ęuə͜r*	our
philosophre	*filosofə͜r*	philosopher
sterre	*stā͜r*	star
theatre	*þiĕtə͜r*	theatre.

* Note: When a word ending with *r* precedes one beginning with a vowel, the *r* is sounded strongly as in a medial position before a

vowel. Moreover an *r* is often inserted between two words in a sentence, when the first ends and the second begins with a vowel, or even weakly sounded after a word ending in a vowel, even when no word beginning with a vowel follows. Examples:

a) *ə'rt gūin t(ə) ǫuər-aus?* = "Are you going to our house?"

b) *ī wontid tə borə'r ə šilin ətū* = "he wanted to borrow a shilling or two."

c) *wīv got ə bǫ-n-arə'r* = "we have got a bow and arrow."

Appendix.

ṭ, *ḍ*.

ME. *ṭi, ḍi* do not become *tš, dž* in the OD., except some forms influenced by the lit. language (cp. Horn, Unters. p. 86 and following).

ME.	OD.	NE.
creatüre	*krētə'r,* *krētḍə'r*	creature
fortüne	*fǫ'rtin* (*fä'rtin*)	fortune
fournitüre	*fornitžə'r*	furniture
natüre	*nētə'r,* *nētḍə'r*	nature
pictüre	*piktə'r*	picture

ME.	OD.	NE.
ruptüre	*rəptə'r,* *rəpšə'r*	rupture
Scriptüre	*Scripšə'r*	Scripture
(ad)ventüre	*ventə'r,* *ventḍə'r*	venture
questioun	*kwestjən,* *kwestšən*	question
tune	*tjūn, tšūn*	tune
soudiour	*sāudžə'r,* *sōdžə'r*	soldier
Indian	*Indžən*	Indian.

Note: For *duke* &c. cp. § 33.

III. GUTTURALS.

k.

§ 97.

I. Initially.

α) *k* preserved, except in certain combinations.

ME.	OD.	NE.
calf	*kǭv*	calf
can	*kon*	can
cǭld	*kaud*	cold
crẹ̄pe	*krīp*	creep

ME.	OD.	NE.
keie	*kē'i*	key
kilne	*kil*	kiln.

β) *k* is dropped before *n* as in lit. English.

knēde	*nē'd, nīd*	knead
knẹ̄	*nī*	knee

ME.	OD.	NE.
knọwe	nọ	know
knīf	nuif	knife.

γ) kl > tl.

clemmen	tlam, tlem	to famish
clẹne	tlīen	clean
clọth	tlọþ	cloth
cloude	tlẹud	cloud
clokke	tlok	clock
clout	tlẹut	rag.

δ) ME. *kw* (*qu*) has mostly been preserved in the OD. — It occurs initially and medially.

1. *kw* preserved.

quāke	kwēk	quake
qvalitē	kwaliti	quality
qvarter	kwārtđər	quarter
quasi	kwīzi	qualmish
quēn	kwīn	queen
qvuestioun	kweštən	question
qviēte	kwəiət	quiet
quishin	kwīšin	cushion.
(OFr. cuissin)		

2. In a few isolated cases initial *kw* > *w* or *tw*.

| quick | wik | quick, live |
| quilte | twilt | quilt (of a bed). |

II. Medially.

α) *kw* preserved (cp. I, δ).

acqueinte	əkwēnt	acquaint
begvẹthe	bikwīđ	bequeathe
consequent	konsi-	conse-
	kwens	quence
egval	ēkwil	equal
requīren	rikwəiər	require.

β) *k* preserved.

ME.	OD.	NE.
scabbe	skab	scab
scars	skārs	scarce
scurf	skrūf	scurf
aker	akər	acre
acorn	akərn	acorn
because	bikoz	because
licour	likər	liguor
huckstere	ukstər	huckster
encrees	inkrīs	increase.

γ) kl > tl (cp. I, γ).

inclinen	intləin	incline
cokel	kotl	cockle
pikel + s	pitlz	pickles
sikel	sitl	sickle
twincle	twintl	twinkle.

Note: The following hyper-literary forms are occasionally found in the OD.

botel	bokl	bottle
ketel	kek(e)l	kettle
litel	likl	little.

δ) *k* dropped before *ed*.

| croked | krūt | crooked. |

ε) *k* dropped between *s* and *l*.

| muscle | musl | muscle. |

III. Finally (ME. and NE) *k* always remains.

brọk	brŭk	brook
nọk	nŭk	nook
ọk	ọk	oak
quick	kwik	quick
bāke	bēk (bak)	bake
māke	mēk, mak	make
tāke	tek, tak	take
walke	wọk	walk.

g.

§ 98.

ME. *g* has remained un-changed, except initially before *l* and *n*.

I. Initially.

α) *g* preserved.

ME.	OD.	NE.
gamen	*gaṃ*	fun
gọ̄ld	*gaud*	gold
gras	*gras, gə̄ʳs*	gräss
girl, gerl	*gə̄ʳl*	girl
gesse	*ges*	guess.

β) *gl* > *dl*.

glad	*dlad*	glad
glas	*dlas*	glass
glorie	*dlọ̄ri*	glory
gloppned	*dlopnt*	terrified
glenten	*dlent*	a look, glance.

γ) *g* is dropped before *n*.

gnawe	*nǭ*	gnaw
gnat	*nat*	gnat

ME.	OD.	NE.
(gnarl)	*nārl*	gnarl
gnaste	*naš*	gnash.

Note: The following words are of Scandinavian origin:

gift	gift
git	get
giv	give
forget	forget
fəʳgiv	forgive.

II. Medially *g* is preserved.

agọ̄(n)	*əgọ̄*	ago
beginne	*bigin*	begin
forget	*fəʳget*	forget
agrée	*əgrī*	agree
bügle	*bjūgl*	bugle
ǧingle	*dẓiŋgl*	jingle.

III. Finally *g* is preserved.

fig	*fig*	fig
leg	*leg*	leg
bagge	*bag*	bag
nagge	*nag*	horse
pegge	*peg*	peg.

χ́ (*ich*-laut).

§ 99.

ME. χ́ has disappeared, the preceding vowel being lengthened:

ME.	OD.	NE
bright	*brīt*	bright
fight	*fē͡it*	fight
light	*līt*	light

ME.	OD.	NE.
night	*nīt*	night
right	*rīt*	right
sight	*sīt*	sight
weight	*wē͡it*	weight.

χ (*ach*-laut).

§ 100.

ME. *gh* occurs medially and finally.

I. Medially.

α) ME. *gh* has dropped before *t*.

ME.	OD.	NE.
aught	*aut*	aught
broȝte	*braut*	brought
doughter	*dautǝʳ*	daughter
feahte	*faut*	fought
naught	*naut*	naught
naught + y	*nauti*	naughty
slaughter	*slautǝʳ*	slaughter
thought	*þaut*	thought.

β) *gh* + *t* = *ft* in the following.

draught	*drauft* (*draut, drǝit*)	draught.

II. Finally.

1. ME. *gh* appears as *f* or is dropped. Most words in the dialect appear with both forms.

bough (bōw)	*būf, bǝf,* *bū*	bough
chough	*tšauf*	chough
dough	*dauf, dōf* *dof*	dough

ME.	OD.	NE.
dwergh	*dwǭʳf*	dwarf
inōugh	*inūf, inū*	enough
plough (plow)	*plū*	plough
rough	*rūf, rū*	rough
slough	*slǝf, slau*	slough
though	*đǭ* (stressed) *đo* (unstr.)	though
thuruh	*þruf, þrū,*[1] *þrǝf*	through
tough	*tauf*	tough
trogh	*trauf, trǭf*	trough.

Note: The forms of substantives and adjectives without *f* are derived from the oblique cases (cp. Köppel, Archiv 104).

2. The change of OE. χ into *k* is found in:

fl<u>ē</u> (OE. = *flēᶦk, flek* flea.
flēah)

For explanation see Horn, Gutturallaute, p. 94.

y.

§ 101.

I. Initially.

1. ME. ȝ, *y* (*j*) from OE. sources has remained in the OD.

ME.	OD.	NE.
ȝ<u>ē</u>	*je*	ye
ȝ<u>ē</u>	*jai*	yes, yea

ME.	OD.	NE.
ȝelde	*jᵘǝld*	yield
ȝelle	*jel*	yell
ȝelwe	*jalǝ*	yellow
ȝēr	*jᵘǝʳ, jǝʳ*	year
ȝerd	*jaʳd, jǝʳd*	yard
ȝesterday	*jestǝʳdi*	yesterday

---

[1] The form *þruf* (*þrǝf*) is noted by Taylor as obolescent.

ME.	OD.	NE.
ʒet	*jit*	yet
ʒon	*jon*	yon
ʒǫng	*juŋg*	young
ʒure	*jə͂ʳ*	your.

2. Initial ʒ had already disappeared in the ME. period in the following.

icche	*itš*	itch
if	*if*	if

ME.	OD.	NE.
inough	*inūf*	enough
(ʒewaer)	*(ə)waʳ*	aware.
iwar		

II. Medially.

ME. ʒ was lost during the ME. period in:

eʒe, eie	*əi*	eye
flēʒe, flīe	*fləi*	fly
hēh, heigh	*həi*	high
nīne	*nəin*	nine.

ng.

§ 102.

Note: In the OD. ŋ is never found alone, being always followed by *g*, this *g*, when final, being occasionally hardened to *k* under the influence of neighbouring dialects (Ashton).

I. Medially ŋg is retained.

ME.	OD.	NE.
England	*Iŋgloɴd*	England
finger	*fiŋgəʳ*	finger
langage	*laŋgwidě*[1]	language
lengre, lenger	*loŋgəʳ*	longer
singer	*siŋgəʳ*	singer
stronger	*stroŋgəʳ*	stronger.

II. Finally.

a) ME. ŋg is retained in accented syllables.

king	*kiŋg*	king
(lang) long	*loŋg*	long
ring	*riŋg*	ring

ME.	OD.	NE.
(strang) strong	*stroŋg*	strong
thing	*þiŋg*	thing.

Note: Nearly all the above are found also with the ending ŋk, these forms being imported from Ashton. The same remark applies to the words which follow under b).

b) ŋg (final) has become *n* in the present participles of all verbs and in substantives of more than one syllable, i. e. in all unaccented positions.

α)

swilling	*swilin*	swilling
swelowing	*swalərin*	swallowing
werking	*wəʳtšin*	working

β)

ferthing	*fáʳđin*	farthing
lerning	*láʳnin*	learning

---

[1] Concerning the insertion of *w* in *langwidž* cp. Köppel, "Spelling Pronunciations" p. 23, 2.

ME.	OD.	NE.
nothing	*nuþin*	nothing
schilling	*šilin*	shilling.

Also in:

among	*əmūn*	among.

Note: *ŋ* is sometimes wrongly put for *n* at the end of words, cp. *mȩuntiŋg* = mountain, *kə˙ting* (*kə˙tnə˙*) curtain (hyperliterary English).

Similarly *ŋg* has been inserted in the word *miliŋgtə˙i* = military.

§ 103.

ME. *ŋk* remains both medially and finally.

I. Medially.

ME.	OD.	NE.
anker	*oŋkə˙*	anchor
ankel	*oŋk(ə)l*	ankle
conqueren	*koŋkə˙*	conquer
drunken	*druŋkn*	drunken
uncle	*unkl*	uncle.

II. Finally (ME. and NE. final position).

bank	*boŋk*	bank

ME.	OD.	NE.
dank	*daŋk*	dank
monk	*moŋk*	monk
drinke	*driŋk*	drink
sinke	*siŋk*	sink
stinke	*stiŋk*	stink.

In the combination *ngth* the OD. has often *ŋkþ*.

length	*leŋkþ*	length
strength	*streŋkþ*	strength.

IV. ASPIRATE.

h.

§ 104.

ME. *h* has mostly disappeared. — It only occurs initially and medially when sounded at all.*

I. Initially.

ME.	OD.	NE.
happene	*apn*	happen
hēr	*ēə˙*	hair
hero	*īəro*	hero
honest	*onist*	honest

ME.	OD.	NE.
hous	*ȩus*	house
hundred	*undə˙ t,* *undð˙t*	hundred.

* Note: When the word is strongly stressed, an initial *h* is sometimes sounded. Hyperliterary forms with an etymologically unjustifiable *h* are also frequent e. g.:

ME.	OD.	NE.
appel	*hapl*	apple
asse	*has*	ass.

II. Medially.

ME.	OD.	NE.
behāve	*bi-ēᶦv*	behave
behinde	*bi-aind*	behind
	(bihənt)	

ME.	OD.	NE.
enhabiten	*inabit*	inhabit
reherce	*ri-ə̄ᵛs*	rehearse.

Note: Medial *h* is hardly ever sounded.

Note: For the prefixing of *j*, after the dropping of *h*, cp. § 16, 2.

PART. II.

ACCIDENCE.

CHAPTER V.

NOUNS.

I. FORMATION OF THE PLURAL.

§ 105.

a) Ordinary Plural Endings.

The usual method of forming the plural in the OD. is by the addition of *s, z* or *iz*.

1. **Plural in *s*.** Nouns ending in a voiceless consonant other than *s, š*, add *s* to form the plural, e. g.: *brūk* (brook), *brūks*; *kat* (cat), *kats*; *top* (top), *tops*; *rūf* (roof), *rūfs*.

2. **Plural in *z*.** Nouns ending in a vowel or voiced consonant other than *z* or *ž*, add *z* to form the plural, e. g.: *keu* (cow), *keuz*; *fləi* (fly), *fləiz*; *flūə^r* (floor), *flūə^rz*; *kitlin* (kitlen), *kitlinz*.

3. **Plural in *iz*.** Nouns ending in *s, š, z* or *ž* add *iz* to form the plural, e. g.: *las* (lass), *lasiz*; *fēs* (face), *fēsiz* [observe, however, *eus* (house), pl. *euziz*]; *matš* (match), *matšiz*; *nuəz* (nose), *nuəziz*; *bridž* (bridge), *bridžiz*.

b) Final Stem-Sound (Stammauslaut).

1. **Nouns ending in *f* preceded by a vowel or *l* change the *f* into *v*,** e. g.: *ləif* (life), *ləivz*; *nəif* (knife), *nəivz*; *þīf* (thief), *þīvz*; *wəif* (wife), *wəivz*; *wulf* (wolf), *wulvz*. — Exceptions: *ūfs* (hoofs); *rūfs* (roofs); *stafs* (staffs); *tlifs* (cliffs).

Note: Nouns ending in *lf* have changed the *f* into *v* in the Sing. by analogy with the plural, e. g.: *ōv* (half), *ǭvz*; *kǭv* (calf), *kǭvz*.

2. Nouns ending in *þ* sometimes change the *þ* into *đ* (*þ* is usually preserved), e. g.: *mẹup* (mouth), *mẹuđz*; *trẹuþ* (truth), *trẹuđz*; — but *baþ* (bath), *baþs*; *pāþ* (path), *paþs* &c.

Note: The *þ* has dropped in the pl. form *tlōz* (clothes).

c) Plurals formed otherwise than by *s*-suffix.

1. Plurals in *n*. Plurals in *n* are still found in: *ī* (eye), *īn*; *šū* (shoe), *šūn*; *oks* (ox), *oksən*, or *eksən* (almost obsolete, cp. Taylor).

2. Plurals in *ər*. The only one still remaining is: *tsəilt* (child), *tšilđər*.

3. Plurals with "Umlaut": *fut* (foot), *fīt*; *gūs* (goose), *gīs*; *lẹus* (louse), *ləis*; *mẹus* (mouse), *məis*; *tūþ* (tooth), *tīþ*; *man*, *mon* (man), *men*. — Observe: *wumən* (woman), *wimin*.

4. Singular and Plural are alike in the following: *biəs* = beast, beasts[1]; *es* (*as*) = ash, ashes; *fīš* = fish, fishes; *šīp* = sheep.

Nouns expressing time, space, weight, measure and number, when proceded by a cardinal number, have singular and plural alike, e. g.: *fəiv munþ* = five months; *siks wīk* = six weeks; *sevn məil* = seven miles; *þrī tun* = three tons; *ē'it pẹund* = eight pounds; *fōər* (*fẹuər*) *ẹuns* = four ounces; *ten skōər* = ten score; *ilevn jā'rd* = eleven yards, &c.

5. Nouns used only in the plural: *aksinz* (askings) = banns of marriage; *bođəmz* = sediments; *līts* = lights (lungs) of animals; *mēzlz* = measles; *siđər̄z* = scissors; *trẹuziz* = trousers; *tuŋgz* = tongs.

Note: A double plural is found in *galəziz* = braces.

II. FORMATION OF THE GENITIVE.

The Genitive is formed as in the literary language: *ẹuər muđər̄z ẹus* = our mother's house; *jōr wentšiz ats* = your girl's hats.

---

[1] Cp. § 85, III.

CHAPTER VI.
ADJECTIVES.
COMPARISON.
§ 106.

I. Regular Comparison. The Comparative is formed by the addition of *-ər* and the Superlative by that of *-ist* to the Positive. This rule is not confined to adjectives of one or two syllables only as in lit. English, *mūə*, *mūəst* (*mūist*, *mwost*) may also be, and often are used together with the forms in *-ər* and *-ist*, e. g.: *þik — þikər — þikist; krūil — krūilər — krūilist; bjūtiful — bjūtifulər bjūtifulist*.

Any of the above may also be compared with *mūə*, *mūist*, e. g.: *mūə krūil — mūist krūil*; or with *mūə*, *mūist* and the termination *ər*, *-ist*, e. g.: *mūə þikər — mūist þikist* (Contamination; cp. Paul, Principien² p. 139, Horn, Anglia-Beiblatt XVI, 136).

II. 'Irregular' Comparison: *bad, il* (bad, ill) — *wus, wər — wust; far, fər* (far) — *fərđər, fǭrđər — fərđist, fǭrđist; lēt* (late) — *lētər — lētist, lǎst; litl* (little) — *les (littlər) — līəst; moni* (many), *mitš* (much) — *mūə — mūəst, mūist, mwost; nīə* (near), *nəi* (nigh) — *nīərər, nəiər, nǟr — nīərist, nəi-ist, nekst*.

CHAPTER VII.
ARTICLE.
§ 107.

The definite article is *þ*, *đ* or rarely *t'*.

1. *þ* is commonly used before unvoiced consonants, e. g.: *þ'pǟrson* the parson; *i'þtęun* into the town; *þ'pəip* the pipe; *þ'kęu* the cow.
2. *đ* is commonly used before voiced consonants, e. g.: *ətop-eđ-bręu* at the top of the hill; *iđdǟrk* in the dark; *đgardnər* the gardener.
3. *t* is sometimes used, where *þ* might be expected, e. g.: *oftsmel* = off the smell.

The above rules are by no means invariable. Of the three forms, *þ* is much the commonest.

Note 1: The form (*t*)*þ* given by Hargreaves is not found in the OD.

Note 2: In expressions denoting anger or surprise, the fuller forms *đǝ* (or *đi* before vowels) is used, e. g.: *ū đǝ devlz điᵊr?* who the devil is there? *wol đi el āᵗt đᾱin?* what the hell art thou doing?

The indefinitive article is ǝ both before vowels and consonants e. g.: *ǝ ęus* a house, *ǝ mon* a man.

CHAPTER VIII

PRONOUNS.

1. PERSONAL PRONOUNS.

§ 108.

First Person.

	Sing.	Plur.
Nom.	*ā, ǭ* (*a o, ǝ*)	*wi* (*ụs*)
Obj.	*mī*, (*mi*)	*us, uz* (*ǝz*).

Second Person.

Nom.	*đā*, (*đā, đǝ, tǝ*)	*jǭ, jo* (*jǝ*)
Obj.	*đī* (*đi*)	*jǭ, jo* (*jǝ*).

Third Person.

Masc.
   Nom. *ī* (*i*)
   Obj. *im*

Tem.
   Nom. *ū* (*u*)
   Obj. *ǝ̄ᵣ* (*ǝᵣ*)

Neut.
   Nom. *it*
   Obj. *it*

Nom. *đē͞ᵢ* (*đi*)
Obj. *đem, ụm,* (*ǝm 'm*).

Note: In the above Table the forms in brackets are unaccented.

EXAMPLES.

The Nom. Case. — First Person: *o (a) dṳn-nǭ, būt ĭ duz.* = I don't mow, but he does; *gi mi sumət tēt* = give me something to eat; *ū akst mi vīəʳ ĭ wə̄ʳ, an a taud əʳ* = she asked me where he was and I told her. — *wi ianno ev (av) tə nok sə ofn* = we shall not have to knock so often; *mṳn ṳs əs) siŋg. piŋksta?* = must we sing, dost thou think? *iz taud ṳs wi mṳn (mən) jū* = he's told us we must go.

Second Person: *ða mǭʳnd* or *ða mṳn-nə* = thou must not; *Wīəʳ ä̆ʳt(ə) juin?* = Where art thou going (to)? [The form *-ta, -tə* is only enclitic]; *an əni on jə oni on it?* = have any of you any of it? *jo mṳn (mən) tel us (əs)* = you must tell us. — In the dialect the second person singular is still used for ordinary intercourse except to strangers or superiors, though in Oldham *jǭ* and *jo* is not always used even then.

Third Person: For the Masc. Sing there is only one form *ī* whether in accented or unaccented position: e. g. *ī nǭs wot a mīn* = he knows what I mean; *wots ĭ want?* = what does he want? — In the Fem. Sing, OE. *heo* has regularly developed to *ū, (u)* thus *hēo > heŏ* (transposition of accent) > *hǭ > (h)ū*: e. g. *ūz wəʳtšin ət Skots* = she is working at Scott's (mill): *ī taud əʳ əz ū'd əftu (aftu) gū* = he told her she would have to go. — In the Neut. Sing. there is only one form *it* e. g. *mṳn (mən) ṳs giv it im* = must we give it to him? — Plurals: *ðə̄ʳ nŏn sețutəd* = they are not suited (= pleased), *gi(v) it əm* = give it them (thrash them)!

The Objective Case. 1. The Objective is regularly used instead of the Nominative case after the verb "to be" in all persons, sometimes even before it, e. g.: *its mī, ðī, im,* &c. = it is I, thou, he, e. g.: *im ən mi'z palz* = he and I are partners.

2. The Objective case is often used reflexively, e. g.: *iz plĕin im* = he is playing (i. e. out of work), *Kețuəʳ ði dețun wəil u pau ði jūəʳ* = sit down while I cut your hair; *est(ə) dond ði (sen)?* = have you dressed yourself?

3. The Objective case is also used as subject when the subject of the principal sentence is separated from the verb by a subordinate sentence, e. g.: *ðem əz ðā mīnz wə̄ʳnt (woznt) ðīəʳ (ðə̄ʳ) nǭ au.* — Those you mean weren't there at any rate, cp. Sweet NEG. § 1085.

2. POSSESSIVE PRONOUNS.

§ 109.

I. Conjoint. Sing.: *məi (mi), ðā (ði), iz, ə̄ʳ (əʳ).*
Plur.: *ețuəʳ, us, jǭʳ (jəʳ), ðə̄ʳ (ðəʳ).*

The forms in brackets are the unaccented ones.

Note: Hargreaves has a form *wəʳ* as unaccented form of *ețuəʳ*, but I have never come across it in the OD.

EXAMPLES: *ðats məi at* = that's my hat; *tak (tek) ðu traps ən bī of!* = take your things and be off! — *ī saud iz watš ən əʳ brūətš ən ǭ* = he sold

his watch and her brooch as well; *ū livz (wụnz) in ęuə^r ęus* = she lives at our
house: *win bin ētin us poritš* = we have been eating our porridge; *an jo gotn
jə^r (jor) bras, ladz?* = have got your money, lads!

II. Absolute. Sing.: *məin, dəin, iz, ə^rz, its.* Plur.: *ęuə^rz,**
jǭ^rz,* dǣ^rz.*

    * Note: The older forms *euə^rn* and *jǭrn* are now obolescent.

    EXAMPLES: *is dat jǭ^rz?* = is that yours; *jai, its ęuə^rz* = yes, it's ours;
Nęu, il nōn get ə peni ə məin = No, he 'll not get a penny of mine.

3. REFLEXIVE PRONOUNS.
§ 110.

    Sing.: 1. *misél, misén*; 2. *disél, disén*; 3. *iz-sél, iz-sén, ə^rsél,
ə^rsén, itsél (is-sél), itsén (is-sén).*
    Plur.: 1. *ęursél(z), ęursén, us-sél(z), ụs-sén*; 2. *jǭ^rsel(z), jǭ^rsen*;
3. *dǣ^rsélz, dǣ^rsén.*
    The Accent is always on the second syllable. The plural forms
can be used with or without the ending *z.*

4. DEMONSTRATIVE PRONOUNS.
§ 111.

    Sing.: *dis* (this); *dat* (that); *jon* (yon).
    Plur.: *dīz* (these); *dem, dūz* (those); *jon* (you); *dis, dīz* are often
followed by *īə^r* = here; *dat, dem* and *dūz* by *dīə^r* = there.

    EXAMPLES: *dis īə^r feli'z gǭmləs* = this fellow here is half-witted; *dem
dīə^r poritəz iznt wup tụpens* = Those potatoes aren't worth twopence. *dem* is
used more frequently than *dūz.*

5. INTERROGATIVE PRONOUNS.
§ 112.

    Masc. and Fem. Nom. Obj.: *uə?* *ū?*   Gen.: *uəz?* *ūz?*
Neut.: *wot? witš* ?

    EXAMPLES: *ūz dīə^r?* who is there? *ūz iz it?* *its nōn Bilz.* = Whose is
it, it is not Bill's; *witš wiltə ev (av)?* Which will you have?

6. RELATIVE PRONOUNS.
§ 113.

    Masc. and Fem.: *əz, u(ə), wot.* Neut.: *əz, wot.*
    When the antecedent is not expressed, *u (uə)* and *wot* are used, e. g.:
tak (tek) wot dəs(t) got = take what you've got; *ī nǭs ū ī mụn gi(v) it tu* =
he knows who he must give it to.

When the antecedent is expressed, *əz* and *wot* are used for all genders, e. g.: *it wər sē'm las əz a sid əfūə* = it was the same lass that I saw before; *im wot taud mi* = he that told me; *ðəm keuz əz wər saud* = those cows that were sold.

7. INDEFINITE PRONOUNS.

§ 114.

sum (some), *sumbri* (somebody), *sumət* (something), *ənūf, ənū* (enough), *tupri* (a few), *evri, ivri* (every), *ǫ* (all), *ani* (any), *anibri* (anybody), *moni* (many), *tǫn* (the one of two), *aut* (anything), *naut* (nothing), *els* (else), *sitš* (such), *ǫðər, ē'ðər* (either), *nǫðər* (neither), *uðər* (other), *nǫ* (no), *nǫn* (none, often used in sense of not).

CHAPTER IX.

NUMERALS.

§ 115.

Cardinals: *won, tū, þrī, fǭər, fəiv, siks, sevn, ait (ē't), nəin, ten, (i)levn, twelv, þə̄rtin (þārtīn), fǭərtīn, fiftīn, undə̄t, ðeusənt.*

Ordinals: *fust (fost), seknd, þə̄rd (þārd), fǭrþ, fift, sikst, sevnt, ēitð*, &c.

Adverbial Numerals: *wonts, twəis, þrəis, þri təimz, fǭər təims.*

In Composition we have *tupri* = "two or three", i. e. a few: *Ūz gotn ə tupri peund sumwīə* = she's got a few pounds somewhere.

CHAPTER X.

VERBS.

I. FORMATION OF TENSES.

A. STRONG VERBS.

§ 116.

Strong Verbs from their Preterite by Ablaut (Gradation). Following the example of Wright and Hargreaves, I have arranged them as far as possible into classes as in Sievers' "A. S. Grammar".

8*

Class I.
§ 117.

Inf.	Pret. Sing.	Pret. Plur.	Past. Part.
OE. *ī*	*ā*	*i*	*i*
ME. *ī*	*ǭ*	*i*	*i*
(h)əid (hide)	*(h)ud*		*hud*
bəit (bite)	*bōt*		*bōt, bitn.*
drəiv (drive)	*drōv*		*drivn*
rəid (ride)	*rōd*		*ridn*
rəit (write)	*rōt*		*rōt, ritn*
rəiv (rive)	*rōv*		*rivn*
rəiz (risze)	*roz*		*riz*
strəid (stride)	*strōd*		*stridn*
strəik, sprəik (strike)	*struk, strok*		*strok, strukn*
šit (cacare)	*šit*		*šitn*
þrəiv (thrive)	*þrov*		*þrivn.*

Note: *əid* (OE. *hȳdan*) was weak in OE. — *dəiv* = dive which is given by Hargreaves as strong in this list is weak in OD. [Pret. *dəift*, P. P. *dəift*] as it was also in OE. — *rəiv* [ME. *riven*] is of Scand. origin and also *þrəiv* [ME. *þrīven*], cp. Björkman, p. 224.

Class II.
§ 118.

Inf.	Pret. Sing.	Pret. Plur.	Past. Part.
OE. *ēo*	*ēa*	*u*	*o*
ME. *ę̄*	*ę̄*	*ǭ*	*ǭ*

Inf.	Pret.	Past. Part.
flāə, fləi (fly)	*flū*	*flaun*
frīz (freeze)	*frōz*	*frozn*
krīp (creep)	*krōp*	*kropn, krōp*
šut (shoot)	*šot*	*šot*
tšūz (choose)	*tšōz*	*tšozn.*

Class III.
§ 119.

This Class had three divisions in OE.: 1. Verbs having a Nasal + Cons., 2. *l* + Cons., 3. *r, h* + Cons. All the verbs originally belonging to 2. have become weak. In subdivision 3. the only strong forms remaining are *fəit* (fight), *brast* (burst).

Inf.	Pret. Sing.	Pret. Plur.	Past. Part.
OE. *i*	*a, o*	*u*	*u*
ME. *i*	*ă, ŏ*	*u, o*	*u, o, ou.*

Inf.	Pret.	Past. Part.
a)		
bigin (begin)	*bigun*	*bigun*
bəind (bind)	*bųn(d)*	*bųn(d)*
briŋg (bring)	*braut*	*braut*
fəind (find)	*fųn(d), fon*	*fųn(d), fon*
grəind (grind)	*grųn*	*grųn*
run (run)	*run*	*run*
spin (spin)	*spųn*	*spųn*
swim (swim)	*swųm*	*swųm*
win (win)	*wųn, wan*	*wųn*
b)		
driŋgk, dɑ̆riŋk (drink)	*drųŋk (draŋk)*	*drųŋk(n)*
riŋg (ring)	*rųŋg (raŋg)*	*rųŋg*
siŋg (sink)	*suŋg*	*sųŋg*
siŋk (sink)	*suŋk*	*sųŋk(n)*
sliŋk (slink)	*sluŋk*	*sluŋk*
spriŋg (spring)	*sprųŋg*	*sprųng*
stiŋg (sting)	*stųŋg*	*stųŋg*
stiŋk (stink)	*stųŋk, staŋk*	*stųŋk*
swiŋg (swing)	*swųŋg*	*swųŋg*
tliŋg (cling)	*tlųŋg*	*tlųŋg*
šrıŋk (shrink)	*šrųnk (šraŋk)*	*šrųnk.*
fəit (fight)	*faut*	*faut, fautn*
brɑst (burst)	*brastid*	*(brastid) brosn.*

Class IV.

§ 120.

Inf.	Pret. Sing.	Pret. Plur.	Past. Part.
OE. *e*	*æ*	*ǣ*	*o*
ME. *ę̄, e*	*a*	*ę̄*	*ǭ*

Inf.	Pret.	Past. Part.
brēᵇk (break)	*brōk*	*broken*
štēᵇl (steal)	*stūl* *	*staun* *
tēʳ (tear)	*tōr, tōʳt* *	*tōʳn*
wēəʳ (wear) *	*wōr*	*wōr, wǭʳn.*

* Note: *wēəʳ* (OE. *werian*) was originally weak. — Peculiar is the form *stūl* which is not found in the Adlington Dialect. — *tort* is a weak-strong form.

kų̄m (come)	*kų̄m*	*komn, kų̆mn.*

komn (*kų̆mn*) has preserved its ME. ending in the OD. which it has lost in the neighbouring dialects.

Class V.
§ 121.

Inf.	Pret. Sing.	Pret. Plur.	Past. Part.
OE. *e*	*æ*	*ǣ*	*e*
ME. *ę̄, ę̇*	*a*	*ę̄*	*ę̄.*

Inf.	Pret.	Past. Part.

1.

nēⁱd (need)	*nēⁱdid, nēⁱdəd*	*nēⁱdəd*
spēⁱk (speak)	*spōk*	*spokn*
trēⁱd (tread)	*trōd*	*trodn*
wēⁱv (weave)	*weⁱvd, wēⁱft*	*wovn*
ēⁱt (eat)	*īt*	*et(ə)n.*

2.

get (get)	*gīt*	*getn*
gi, giv (give)	*gan*	*gan*
sī (see)	*sīd*	*sīn (sin)*
sit (sit)	*sit*	*sit**
stik (stick)*	*stụk*	*stukn*
dig (dig)*	*dụg*	*dụg(n).*

* Note: These two verbs were weak in OE. — The form *sīt* for *sit* P.P. is obsolete in the OD.

Class VI.
§ 122.

Inf.	Pret. Sing.	Pret. Plur.	Past. Part.
OE. *a*	*ō*	*ō*	*a*
ME. *ā*	*ǭ*	*ǭ*	*a.*

Inf.	Pret.	Past. Part.
drēⁱ, drǭ (draw)	*drū*	*drǭn*
stōnd (stand)	*stụd*	*stụd(n)*
tek, tak (take)	*tūk*	*takn, tēn*
swə̄ʳ (swear)	*swōə̄ʳ*	*swǭʳn.*

Class VII (Reduplicating Verbs).
§ 123.

uŋg (hang)	*uŋg*	*uŋg*
let (let)	*let, līt*	*letn*
fǭ (fall)	*fōd*	*fōn (fōd)*
bjet (beat)	*bīt*	*bjetn*
grū (grow)	*grū*	*grūn*
blō (blow)	*blū, blōd*	*blōn*
mō (mow)	*mōd*	*mōn*
nō (know)	*njū, nōd*	*nōn, nōd.*

B. WEAK VERBS.

I. Preterite and Past Participle in əd (id).

Inf.	Pret.	P. P.
fret (fret)	*frĕtəd (frĕtid)*	*frĕtəd*
lit (light)	*lītid (let)*	*lītid (let)*
melt (melt)	*meltəd*	*meltəd*
sūt (suit)	*sūtəd (sūtid)*	*sūtəd (sūtid)*
trēt (treat)	*trētəd (trētid)*	*trētəd (trētid)*
wīt (wet)	*wītəd*	*wītəd*
aud (hold)	*auded*	*audəd.*

II. Preterite and Past Participle in d.

a) Verbs in which the vowel remains unchanged:

brū (brew)	*brud*	*brūd*
īər (hear)	*īərd*	*īərd*
lē, lī (lay)	*lēd*	*lēd*
mak (make)	*mēd*	*mēd*
rū (rue)	*rūd*	*rūd*
sē, se (say)	*sed*	*sed*
sō (sow, sew)	*sōd*	*sōn*
šō (shew)	*šōd*	*šōn*
šū (shoe)	*šūd*	*šud*
tšū (chew)	*tšūd*	*tsūd.*

b) Verbs which change the vowel and add d to the stem:

sel (sell)	*saud*	*saud*
tel (tell)	*taud*	*taud*
tīm (teem, pour out)	*temd*	*temd.*

c) Verbs which change the vowel and have d in the stem:

blīd (bleed)	*bled*	*bled*
brīd (breed)	*bred*	*bred*
fīd (feed)	*fed.*	*fed.*

III. Preterite and Past Participle in -t.

a) Verbs with unchanged vowel and original t, d in the stem:
1.

it (hit)	*it*	*it*
kost (cost)	*kost*	*kost*
kut (cut)	*kut*	*kut*
nit (knit)	*nit*	*nit*
oᵣt, əᵣt (hurt)	*oᵣt, əᵣt*	*ort, əᵣt*
put, pət (put)	*put, pət*	*put, pət*
swīət (sweat)	*swet*	*swet.*

Note: *swīət* seems to he an importation from Yorkshire, cp. Wright § 381.

Inf.	Pret.	Past. Part.
2.		
bend (bend)	*bent*	*bent*
bild (build)	*bilt*	*bilt*
send (send)	*sent*	*sent*
skrat (scratch)	*skrat*	*skrat*
spend (spend)	*spent*	*spent.*
3.		
wed (wed)	*wed*	*wed.*

b) Verbs with unchanged vowel which add *t* to the stem:

1.		
elp (help)	*elpt*	*elpt*
katš (catcb)	*katš*	*katšt*
kis (kiss)	*kist*	*kist*
rētš (reach)	*rētšt*	*rētšt*
sītš (seek)	*sītšt*	*sītšt*
šēk (shake)	*šēkt*	*šēkt*
šēp — šap (shape)	*šapt*	*šapt*
šēv (shave)	*šēft*	*šēft*
wēiš (wash)	*wēⁱšt*	*wēⁱšt*
wəʳtš (work)	*wəʳtšt*	*wəʳtšt.*
2.		
brųn (burn)	*brųnt*	*brųnt*
lan(d) (lend)	*lant*	*lant*
līən (lean)	*lēⁱnt*	*lēⁱnt*
smel (smell)	*smelt*	*smelt*
spel (spell)	*spelt*	*spelt*
spɪl (spill)	*spilt*	*spilt*
spəil (spoil)	*spəilt*	*spəilt*
šəin (shine)	*šəint*	*šəint*
wakn (waken)	*waknt*	*waknt.*

c) Verbs with Vowel Change and original *t* in stem:

mīt (meet)	*met*	*met.*

d) Verbs with Vowel Change which add *t* to the stem:

bəi (buy)	*baut*	*baut*
briŋg (bring)	*braut*	*braut*
drīəm, ðrīəm (dream)	*dremt, ðremt*	*dremt, ðremt*
fɪl (feel)	*felt*	*felt*
kīp (keep)	*kept*	*kept*
līəv (leave)	*laft*	*laft*
lūz, lōz (lose)	*lost*	*lost*
mīən (mean)	*ment*	*ment*
nīl (kneel)	*nelt*	*nelt*

Inf.	Pret.	Past. Part.
pīp (peep)	*pept*	*pept*
slīp (sleep)	*slept*	*slept*
swīp (sweep)	*swept*	*swept*
tē͏ᵢts (teach)	*tē͏ᵢtst (taut)*	*tē͏ᵢtšt (taut)*
þiŋk (think)	*þaut*	*þaut.*

II. VERBAL ENDINGS.

§ 124.

Present. The first person singular has no ending, the second and third person singular ends in *s* (after voiced sounds *z*) and *is* or *iz* after the spirants *s, z, š, ž*. The plural mostly ends in *ən* throughout, but the first and third person are sometimes the same as the third person singular, while the second person has no ending.

Present Sing.	1.	*elp (help)*	*wəʳtš (work)*
	2.	*elps*	*wəʳtšəz*
	3.	*elps*	*wəʳtšəz*
Plur.	1.	*elpən (elps)*	*wəʳtšən (wəʳtšəz)*
	2.	*elpən (elp)*	*wəʳtšən (wəʳtš)*
	3.	*elpən (elps)*	*wəʳtšən (wəʳtšəz)*
Preterite		*elpt*	*wəʳtšt*
Imperative		*elp*	*wəʳtš*
Infinitive		*elp*	*wəʳtš*
Present Participle		*elpin**	*wəʳtšin**
Past Participle		*elpt*	*wəʳtšt.*

* For *-in* < *ing* in the Pres. Participle, cp. § 62, IIb.

The **Subjunctive Mood** has disappeared except in certain phrases, e. g. *"if a (o) wəʳ dī"* = "if I were you". The future, the perfect tenses and the passive voices are formed as in literary English.

Table of Tenses.

Tense	Indefinite	Imperfect and Continuous	Perfect	Perfect and Continuous
Present	$\left.\begin{array}{l}a\\o\end{array}\right\}$ $wə^rt\check{s}$ = I work	$\left.\begin{array}{l}am\\om\end{array}\right\}wə^rt\check{s}in$ = I am working	$\left.\begin{array}{l}av\\ov\end{array}\right\}$ $wə^rt\check{s}t$ = I have worked	$\left.\begin{array}{l}av\\ov\end{array}\right\}bin\ wə^rt\check{s}in$ =I have been working
Preterite	$\left.\begin{array}{l}a\\o\end{array}\right\}$ $wə^rt\check{s}t$ = I worked	$\left.\begin{array}{l}a\\o\end{array}\right\}$ $wə^r\ wə^rt\check{s}in$ $\bar{ǫ}ə^r$ $wə^rt\check{s}in$ = I was working	$ad\ wə^rt\check{s}t$ = I had worked	$ad\ bin\ wə^rt\check{s}in$ = I had working
Future	$\left.\begin{array}{l}as\\os\end{array}\right\}$ $wə^rt\check{s}$ = I shall work	$\left.\begin{array}{l}as\\os\end{array}\right\}$ $bi(n)$ $wə^rt\check{s}in$ = I shall be working	$\left.\begin{array}{l}as\ e\\os\ ə\end{array}\right\}$ $wə^rt\check{s}t$ $os(t)\ ə\ wə^rt\check{s}t$ =I shall have worked	$\left.\begin{array}{l}as\ e\\os\ ə\end{array}\right\}bin\,wə^rt\check{s}in$ $os(t)\ ə\ bin$ $wə^rt\check{s}in$ = I shall have been working

Notes: In the OD. a *t* is inserted in the Future Perfect and the Fut.
Perf. and Continuous Tenses. This does not appear to be the case in neighbouring dialects. —

The ending of the 3rd pers. Sing is used with plural nouns, expecially in a relative clause, e. g.: *ðem əz ləiks kon av mūə^r* = those who like can have more. — *ðin ǫ getn wed* = they are all getting wed (married); *a kud ləik tə si wot sǭə^rtə stuf ðə driŋkən* = I should like to see what sort of stuff they drink? After the personal pronouns the ending -*ən* is always used: *ðə plēin fut-bǭ ivri deᶦ* = they play football every day.

The literary English form without ending for the 3rd pers. pl. is also found thus: *ðe wə^rtš ət Plats* = they work at Platts (a large Oldham iron-works).

ANOMALOUS VERBS.
1. Can.
Pres. Strong form *kon*, weak form *kn*.
Pret. Strong form *kud*, weak form *kəd*.

Affirmatively.
Present.
Sing. 1. *a, o, kon* or *kn*.   Plur. *wi kon* or *kn*.
2. *ða kon* or *kn*.   *jo, jə kon* or *kn*.
3. *ī, ū, it kon* or *kn*.   *ðe, ði kon* or *kn*.

Preterite.

Pret. *kud* or *kəd*
&c.

kud or *kəd*
&c.

Negatively.

Pres. *a, o konət* or (*kǭʳnd*)*   Pret. *a, o kudnd(t).*

Note: In Oldham proper the forms are *konət* and *kudnt*, in Hollinwood, a southern suburb, *konəʳ* and *kudnəʳ*. The form *kǭʳnd* is rare.

Interrogatively.

Present.

Sing. 1. *kon* (or *kn*) *a?*   Plur. *kon* (or *kn*) *wi, us, əs?*
     2. *kon* (or *kn*) *đa, tə?**   *kon* (or *kn*) *jo, jə?*
     3. *kon* (or *kn*) *ī, ū, it?*   *kon* (or *kn*) *đē, đi, đe?*

* Note: The enclitic form *tə* is the one preferred in Oldham.

Interrogative-Negatively.

   1. *konət a, o?*   *konət wi?*
   2. *kontno?**   *konət jo, je?*
   3. *kont* *ī ū, it?*   *konət đē, đi, đə?*

* Note: The contracted forms in the 2nd and 3rd pers. Sing.

kud is sometimes used in the Infinitive e. g.: *a jūs tə kud* = "I used to be able (to do it)".

2. Dare.

Pres.	Pret.
a də̄ʳ = I dare	*a də̄ʳ* = I dared
a dəʳnt, dəʳnə = I dare not	*a də̄ʳsnt* = I dare not
də̄ʳa? = dare I	*də̄ʳa?* = dared I
dəʳnt, dəʳsnt a? = dare I not.	*dəʳsnt a?* did I not dare?

The preterite and past participle *də̄ʳd* = challenged, e. g.: *ī də̄ʳd im tə kụm ęut ən fəit* = he challenged him to come out and fight.

3. Shall.

Present-Affirmatively.

Sing.	Plur.
1. *a, o, šal* (form *as, os*)	*wi šal* (weak form *wis* [*t* before vowel])*
2. *đa, đə šal* (*đas*)	*jə šul* or *šan* (*jəs*)
3. *ī, ū, šal, šul* (*īs, us*)	*đi, đe šal, šul, šan* (*đis*).

* Note: In the first pers. plural of the affirmative form the strong form seldom occurs.

Negatively.

Sing.	Plur.
a, o šanə, &c.	*wi šanə, &c.*

Interrogatively.

1. *šal a, o?*	*šal* or *šan wi, uə, əs?*
2. *saltə?*	*šal* or *šan jo, jə?*
3. *šal ī, ū?*	*šal* or *šan đē, đi, đe?*

In the plural the form *šan* is preferred.

Interrogative-Negatively.

šanət a, o? &c.	*šanə(t) wi, us, əs? &c.*

Preterite. Affirmatively.

a, o šud, šəd	*wi šud, šəd*
đa šud, šəd	*jo, jə šud, šəd*
ī, ū, it šud, šəd	*đə, đi šud, šəd.*

Negatively.

a, o šudnt, šədnt &c.	*wi šudnt, šədnt &c.*

Interrogatively.

šud, šəd a, o? &c.	*šud, šəd wi, us, əs? &c.*

Negative-Interrogatively.

šudnt, šədnt a? &c.	*šudnt, šədnt wi? &c.*

The weak forms are generally used only with pronouns.

4. May.

Present.

a me (mi) &c.	*wi me (mi) &c.*

Preterite.

a met &c.	*wi met &c.*

Note: The use of *kon* for *me* in the present, found in the neighbouring dialect, does not extend to Oldham (cp. Hargreaves, § 116).

For the Interrogative *mon, mun, mən* is used for the Present tense, e. g.:

Sing.	Plur.
mon a? &c.	*mon (mun, mən) wi, us, əs &c.*

e. g.: *mən əs siŋg, þiŋksta?* = may (or shall) we sing, do you think?

Preterite.

met a? &c.	*met wi &c.*

Negatively.

Sing.

a mənə (I may, must not)

mənət a?

Plur.

wi mənə

mənə(t) wi?

Note: The Adlington form *mutnt* is not found in the OD., cp. Hargreaves § 116.

5. Must.

To express the lit. Engl. *must*, the Scandinavian *munn, mann* is used: strong form *mon*, weak form *mun, mən* the forms of the first person singular and plural are as follows:

Sing.

a, o mon (*mun, mən*)

a, o mənə (I must not)

mon, mən a? (must I?)

mənət a, o? (must I not?)

Plur.

wi mon

wi mənə

mən əs?

mənət əs?

Note: The Adlington form *mǭ'nd* is rare in the OD. Also the weak form *mən* is regularly used negatively.

For the Preterite the same forms are used as above, but the form *met* is also used occasionally in the same sense.

6. ought.

aut is uninflected for all persons; observe: *a autnt* or *didnt aut* = I ought not; *autnt a* or *didnt a aut?* = ought I not?

7. Have.

Pres. Strong Form *av, a, an*; weak *əv, ə, ən*.

Pret. Strong Form *ad*; weak *əd*.

Before consonants the form *a* or *ə* are always used, tho' *ə* is commoner, e. g.: *əs a* (*ə*) *dŭn inau* = I shall have done presently; but *il av it əfuə' əts lŭŋg* = he will have it before (its) long. —

In both Pres. and Pret. the vowels disappear in the weak forms when preceded by the nominative of the personal pronouns, e. g.: *ǭv* = I have. *win* = we have; *ad sin im* = I had seen him. Sometimes the verb disappears altogether, e. g.: *ðe mad əm* = they have made them; *wi lost it* = we have lost it. This is the case before vowels mostly cp. *win etn it* = we have eaten it. The *z* of the second and third person singular becomes *s* before voiceless consonants: e. g.: *astə?* = hast thou!

Affirmatively.
Present.
Sing.	Plur.
1. *a av; q̄v*	*wi av; win (wiv)*
2. *đa az; đaz đəz*	*jo av, an; jə̄n, jən*
3. *ī, ū, it az; īz, ūz, its*	*đē, đi, đə av, an; đin.*

Preterite.
1. *a ad; ād, q̄d, əd*	*wi ad; wīd*
2. *đa ad; đād, đad*	&c.

Infinitive *av, a, ə.*
Present Participle *avin.*
Past. Participle *ad, əd.*

Negatively.
Present.
1. *a anə*	*wi anə*
2. *đa, đə aznə*	*jo, jə anə*
3. *ī, ū, it aznə*	*đe anə.*

Preterite.
a adnə	*wi adnə.*

Note: The Adlington forms differ considerably from the above, cp. Hargreaves § 119.

Interrogatively.
Present.
1. *av a?*	*an wi? (av wi?)*
2. *(az đa?) astə?*	*an, av jo, jə?*
3. *az ī, ū, it?*	*an, av đē, đi, đe?*

The *an* form is much commoner in the OD.

Preterite.
ad a? &c.	*ad wi? &c.*

Interrogative-Negatively.
1. *anət a?*	*anə(t) wi? anət wi?*
2. *astnə?*	*anə(t) jo? jə?*
3. *aznt ī, or aznə ī, ū &c.*	*anət đi?*

Preterite.
adnt a? &c.	*adnt wi? &c.*

The Plural forms of the Present given above are only used with the personal pronouns. In all other cases the forms of the second and third person singular are used thus: *az, əz (s)*, e. g.: *az đem wentšəz gun wom?* = have those girls gone home? *đem đīeʳ ladz əz bin fēⁱtin* = those lads have been fighting. The same forms are also used with the first pers. sing when combined with a relative, e. g.: *its mī əz əz fon it* = It was I who found it.

8. Be.

Affirmatively.

Present.

Sing.	Plur.
1. *ă am; ǫm; am*	*wi āʳ, wə̄ʳ, wəʳ*
2. *đa āʳ; đęu, đa aʳt; đəʳt*	*jo, je aʳ; jə̄ʳ, jeʳ*
3. *ī, ū, it iz; īz, ūz, its*	*đē, đi, đe aʳ; đə̄ʳ, đəʳ.*

Preterite.

1. *a wə̄ʳ, wəʳ*	*wī, wi wəʳ, wəʳ* = we were
2. *đa wəʳ(t)*	&c.
3. *ī wə̄ʳ, wəʳ.*	

Infinitive *bī, bi.*
Pres. Part. [*bī·in*].
Past Part. *bin.*

Negatively.

Present.

1. *am, om not, nət or nōn*	*wī, wəʳ not, nət, nōn*
2. *đəʳt not, nət or nōn*	*jōʳ, jəʳ not, nət, nōn*
3. *īz, ūz, its not, nət or nōn*	*đə̄ʳ, đəʳ not, nət, nōn.*

Preterite.

a, o wə̄ʳnt, wəʳnt &c.	*wi, wə̄ʳnt &c.*

Interrogatively.

Present.

1. *am a, o?*	*āʳ wi or ʉs?*
2. *aʳtə? (aʳt đa?)*	*āʳ jo or jə?*
3. *iz, i, ū, it?*	*āʳ đē, đi, đe?*

Preterite.

wə̄ʳ, weʳ a?	*wə̄ʳ, wəʳ wi, us? &c.*
wəʳtə? (wəʳt đa?) &c.	

Interrogative-Negatively.

Present.

1. *amti? amta?*	*aʳnə(t) wi?*
2. *aʳtnə?*	*aʳnt jə (jo)?*
3. *iznə(ʳ)* / *iznt* } *ī, ū, it?*	*aʳnə(t) đi?*

Note: The forms in brackets are the less common. A comparison of these forms with those of Adlington and Windhill show the intermediate stage occupied by the OD. very well.

Preterite.

Sing.	Plur.
wᵊ͞rnt a, o? &c.	*wᵊ͞rnt wi, us?*

The above forms of the present are used only in combination with the pronouns, in other cases the 3ʳᵈ sing is used, e. g.: *đem ęuziz iznt let jet* = those houses are not let yet; *đəʳz sṳm on əm əz duznt nǫ nǭ difrənt* = there are some of them who do not know any better; *đəʳz sṳm feliz əz kn nəvəʳ ẹt inūf* = there are some fellows who can never eat enough.

The Vowel disappears, or is assimilated to the foregoing vowel of the subject in the weak forms of the present, e. g.: *đəʳ at it əgen* = they are at it again — *am (om) nōn redi jet.* = I am not ready yet. —

9. Will.

Present: strong form *wil*, weak *əl*, which loses its vowel in combination with pronouns.

Preterite: strong form *wud*, weak form *əd* which also loses its vowel in combination with the pronouns, e. g.: *ad (od) lan(d) đi ə tupri šilin but a konət dū (djū) bęut it nęu* = I would lend you a shilling or two, but I cannot do without it now.

Affirmatively.

Present.

Sing.	Plur.
1. *a, o wil; al, ǫl, ol*	*wi wil; wīl, wil, win*
2. *đu wil; đaul, đęul*	*jo, jə wil; jəl, jəl, jon*
3. *ī, ū, it wil; īl, ūl, itl*	*đē, đi, đe wil; đēl, đil, del.*

Note: Of the above plural forms *win, jon, đil* are the most used.

Preterite.

a, o wud, wəd; ǫd, ad, əd &c.   *wi wud, wəd; wīd, wid* &c.

Negatively.

Present.

1. *a winə, al nōn*   *wi winə, wil nōn* &c.
2. *đa, đə winə, đal, đəl nōn* &c.

Preterite.

a, o wudnt &c.   *wi wudnt* &c.

Interrogatively.

Present.

	Sing.	Plur.
1.	*wil a, o?*	*win wi?*
2.	*wilta, wiltə?*	*win jo, jə?*
3.	*wil ī, ū, it?*	*win di?*

Preterite.

1.	*wud a, o?*	*wud wi, us, əs?*
2.	*wud da, tə? &c.*	*wud jo, jə &c.*

Interrogative-Negatively.

Present.

1.	*winət, wint a?*	*winət, wint wi?*
2.	*wiltna?*	*winə jə?*
3.	*wint ī, ū, it?*	*winə di?*

Note: The shortened form *wint* is preferred for the 1st and 3rd pers. sing., the form *winət* for the 1st pers. plur., and the form *winə* for the 2nd and 3rd pers. plur.

Preterite.

1. *wudnt a? wədnt a?*	*wudnt wi?*

For the 1st pers Sing. and Plur. in all the interrogative forms, the verb *shall* (q. v.) is sometimes used.

10. Do.

do as an independent verb is conjugated like any other verb. In the Preterite *did* is used for all persons Sing. and Plur.

Affirmatively.

Present.

1.	*a dŭ?*	*wi*	
2.	*da duz*	*jo, jə*	*dŭ, dun.*
3.	*ī, ū, it du(z)*	*dē, di*	

Negatively.

1.	*a dǭrnt, dərnt*	*wi*	
2.	*da duznt*	*jo, jə*	*dǭrnt, dərnt.*
3.	*ī, ū, it duznt*	*dē, di*	

Interrogatively.

Sing.   Plur.

1. *dū a, o?*
2. *duz d̆a? dust(ə)?*   *dun, dən* { *wi?*
3. *duz ī, ū, it?*   *jo, jə?*
                                                      d̆ē, d̆i?

Interrogative-Negatively.

dunət a? dōᵣnt a?   *dunət wi &c.*
duznt d̆a? dunət na?
duznt, dunət ī, ū, it?

Pres. Part.: *duin.*

Past. Part.: *dun, dən.*

In the form *dustə* = dost thou? the *ə* is sometimes dropped
before consonants thus *dust nō?* = dost thou know?

Note: The Verb *do* is not used so frequently to ask questions as in literary
English, e. g.: *šud a siŋg, þiŋksta?* = should I sing, dost thou think?

Appendix.

ADVERBS.

§ 125.

Adverbs of Manner and Degree mostly end in *-li*, e. g.:
aᵣdli = hardly, *ǫkəᵣtli* = awkwardly. In *suəᵣlī* the stress is on the
suffix.

apn = perhaps; *ęu* = how; *ęu-iver* = however; *ən ǭ (ǭ)* =
and all, too, as well.

Notes: 1. On the use of *ęu: a dųnŏ ez ęu 'it matəᵣz* = I don't think it is
of much consequence.

In interrogative sentences "how" is often replaced by *witš
rǭd?* thus *witš rǭd (rǭd) mən əs bigin?* = how must we begin?

2. On the use of *ən ǭ (ǭ): ī wil d̆at ən ǭ* = "he will that, and no
mistake" (strengthening sense).

ǭləz, ǭləz = **always**; *tū* = too, also; *sǭ (sǭ)* = so, but *ū wəᵣ
d̆at mad* = she was so angry.

veri = very, often replaced by *sųm* thus: *ī wəᵣ sųm mad, ī
wə̄ᵣ* = he was very angry (that) he was; *veri nīəᵣ* almost, *wəi?* =
why? *wīl* = well (Interjection *wəl!*)

"Also" is expressed, as seen above, by *tu* and *ən ǭ*. "Thus"
by *d̆is rǭd,* or *d̆at rǭd* = "this road" or "that road".

Adverbs of Place: *oniwīə^r* = anywhere; *īə^r* = here; *jon* = yonder; *sumwīə^r* = somewhere; *dīə^r (d̄ə^r)* = there; *wīə^r (wə̄^r)* = where?

Adverbs of Time: *evə^r*, *ivə^r* = ever; *jet* = yet; *justə^rdĕⁱ* *(jusþə^rdĕⁱ)* = yesterday; *nęu* = now; *nivə^r* = never; *oft* = often; *sin* = since; *sūn* = soon; *tədēⁱ* = to-day; *təmq̄^rn (t'mō^rn)* = to-morrow; *tənīt (t'nīt)* = to-night; *đen* = then; *inau* = presently; *wen* = when.

Affirmative and Negative Particles: *ai*, *jai*, *a* = yes; *nāu*, *nęu* (stressed) *nō* (unstr.) = no; *nōn*, *not* = not (also *nət*, *nt* when unstressed).

PREPOSITIONS.

§ 126.

aftə^r (afđə^r) = after; *əfōə^r*, *əfūə^r* = before; *bi* = by; *bi-int*, *bihənt* = behind; *dęun* = down; *ə*, *əv* (only before vowels) = of; *əbęut* = about; *bęut* = without; *əbūn* = above; *əgen* = again; *əgin* = against; *əlуŋg* = along; *əmuŋg* = among; *bisəid* = besides; *əstid ə* = instead of; *fə^r* = for; *frə* = from; *in*, *i* = in (*i* is more used, even before vowels); *intə* = into; *nīə^r*, *nəi* = near; *but obət* = except [*obə^r* in Hollinwood, see map]; *nobət*, *nobə^r* (Holl.) = *only*; *on*, *o* = on; *oə^r* = over; *sin* = since; *tə*, *til* = to, as far as (e. g. *wi went veri nīə^r til Audəm* = we went almost as far as Oldham); *þrū (þrəf, þruf)* = through; *undə^r*, *undə^r* = under; *up*, *op* = up; *wi* = with.

CONJUNCTIONS.

§ 127.

but = but; *bikos*, *kos* = because (sometimes *koz*); *ən* = and; *əz* = that (*đat* is never used as a conjunction); *if*, *iv* = if; *nođə^r* *(nǭđə^r)* = neither; *ǭđə^r*, *ōđə^r*, *ēđə^r* = either; *nə^r* = than, always used in comparisons[1] cp. *īz bigə^r nə^r mī* = he is bigger than I; *wəil* = until cp. *wi mən wīt (wet) wəil ī kумz* = we must wait until he comes.

---

[1] For explanation cp. Horn, Archiv CXIV, 360.

SPECIMENS.[1]

I.

Sam o Dukiz Kūᵊʳtšip (Brierley).

Sam. đẹu-ᵊʳt swilin đi kŏt ẹut aud krētᵊʳ.

Mary. iz đat jo, Sam.?

S. ə bit əþaud tᵊʳmit. Ẹu aʳtə, aud wentš?

M. Oın əz rīt əz fǭᵊʳ penəþ ə kopᵊʳ. Ẹu əʳ jo, Sam?

S. Wel, đa sīz, mi tšins getin nāʳ mi gāʳtᵊʳz nᵊʳ it jūstᵊʳbi, on e fil ə bit šĕⁱki opə mi props; bət om sẹund əbẹut'þ hāʳnel ən kwəit lediš əbẹut'þjəd. đa lūks prəim aud damzel. Ẹu əʳþ tšildə'?

M. ē, đin ǭ getin ıved obət ẹuᵊʳ Sērə, ən ūl nō bi luŋg fᵊʳ ūz kūᵊʳtin veri drī.

S. əi, əi, ıvot sūᵊʳt ə səns ən dautᵊʳz in lǭ ast getn? āʳ đe ov ɔ farəntli mak?

M. Midlin. Tū ev ẹuᵊʳ wentšəz ᵊʳ ıved tə koljᵊʳz getin gud wĕⁱdžiz, bət đe kn ĕʳt weli ǭ de getn, ən ẹuᵊʳ Džō əz ıved ə mantimākᵊʳ, bət ū əznə ınitš wāʳk bikoz wentšiz əbẹut ıᵊʳ ən bigən dū.in đᵊʳ ōn sō.ın.

S. ǭ, đᵊʳt getin kwəit əmụŋgþ kwaliti, a jĕʳ, đẹul bi laʳnin tə tǭk fəin nekst ən getin ə tinklin boks iþẹus, đǭ ə þiŋk đəi fiŋgᵊʳz ᵊʳ rĕⁱđᵊʳ tə wāʳk prẹud fᵊʳ tə dū ınitš ıniūsik ə đat sūᵊʳt. Kĕⁱđᵊʳ mjūsik əz bin ınūᵊʳ i đəi rǭd. Wot sūᵊʳt əv ə tšap əz jᵊʳ Sērə getn?

M. ǭ, iz ə kwaliti grĕⁱdli, ẹuᵊʳ Sērə'z feli iz, ī ıvᵊ̄ʳz ə watš ən gəz intə Bāʳ Pāʳlᵊʳz.

S. əi, duz ī ıvᵊ̄ʳ əwatš? A dunə ləik đat. O nivᵊʳ niū ə mon jet ət ıvǭᵊʳ ə watš bət ī ıvent tū fāst, ī ıvᵊʳ sūᵊʳ tə galop wen ī

---

[1] The translations are as nearly literal as possible.

SPECIMENS.

I.

Sam of Ducky's Courtship (Brierley).

S. You are swilling your (pig) sty out, old creature.

M. Is that you, Sam?

S. A bit of the old turnip. How are you, old wench?

M. As right as four penny-worth of copper. How are you, Sam?

S. Well, you see, my chin is getting nearer my garters than it used to be, and I feel a bit shaky upon my props (legs) but I'm sound about the kernel and quite laddish (juvenile) about the head. You look prime, old damsel. How are the children?

M. Eh, they have all got wed (married) but our Sarah, and she will not be long, for she is courting very busily.

S. Yes, yes. What sort of sons and daughters-in-law have you got? Are they of a good make? (= are they respectable).

M. Middling. Two of our wenches are wed to colliers, getting good wages, but they can eat nearly all they get (earn) and our Joe has wed a mantle-maker, but she has not much work because the wenches about here have begun doing their own sewing.

S. Oh, you are getting among the quality (fine folk) I hear, you will be learning to talk fine (speak lit. Engl.) next and (be) getting a tinkling-box (piano) into the house. Though I think your fingers are rather too work-proud for to do much music of that sort. Cradle-music has been more in your road (line). What sort of a chap has your Sarah got?

M. Oh, he's a quality indeed (a grand person) is our Sarah's sweetheart, he wears a watch and goes into Bar Parlours.

S. Oh, does he wear a watch? I don't like that. I never knew a man yet that wore a watch, but (he) went too fast, he was sure to gallop when he should have walked, and get to the

šud ə wǭkt, ən get təþend ev iz bant i nǭ təim, ən az fər gūin
intə Bā̆r Pā̆rlə̆rz, a nivər sǭ mitš sens kɥm ɥut ə đīə̆r. Iv đi
getn ə bit ə jūə̆r opə đə̆r top lip ən ə fəin wə̄rd ə̆r tū i đə̆r
mɥuþ en kn tikəl ə bā̆r mē'd bɥut getin ə klɥut oþ said oþ jed,
đe þinkn đer evribodi wen đēə̆r nǭbdi ətɒ sē'm təim. Om dɥun
on əm spēšli if đə̆r ats iz grēsi ən đə̆r jūə̆r ez əili əz þ'midl
əv ə kā̆rtwīl, ən đə̆r trɥuziz klatə̆rt əđ boþm, ən đə̆r dikiz əbɥut
þ'kolə̆r əv ə mē'ri-gaud ən əz moni riŋgz on đə̆r fiŋgə̆rz əz əd
mak ə d'ǭg-tšiən, o wudno giv ə skǭdin ə krā̆bz fə̆r ə wul kenil-
ful ə sitš-ləik welps.

II.

Kɥm wom tə 'đi tšildə̆r ən mī (Waugh)[1].

1. Ov džust mendid þ'fəiə̆r wi ə kob
   Aud Swadl əz braut đi njū šūn
   də̆rz sum nəis bēkn koləps oþob
   ən ə kwǭrt ə hēl posit iþ ūn
   ov braut đi top kwot dust nǭ
   fe̅r þrēns kumin dɥun veri drī
   ən þā̆rþstuən'z əz wəit əz njū snǭ
   kɥm wom tə đi tšildə̆r en mi.

2. wen a put litl Sali tə bed
   ū krəid koz ə̆r fē'đə̆r wə̆rnt đīə̆r
   sǭ o kist t'litl þiŋg ən o sed
   đad briŋg ə̆r ə ribin froþ fə̄r
   ən o giv ə̆r ə̆r dol en sɥm ragz
   ən ə nəis liţl wəit kotn bǭ
   ən o kist ər əgen; but ū sed
   əz ū wantid tə kis đī ən ǭ.

3. ən Dik tū, ad sitš wa̅rk wi im
   əfūə̆r o kəd get im up stə̆rz;
   đa taud im đed briŋg im ə drɒm

---

[1] The same poem may also to be found in Hargreaves p. 114.

end of his tether in no time, and as for going into Bar Parlours. I never saw much sense come out of there. If they get a bit of hair on the top of their lip and a fine word or two in their mouth and can tickle a bar-maid without getting a blow on the side of the head they think they are everybody when they're nobody at the same time. I'm down on them especially if their hats are greasy (if they use hair-oil) and their hair is as oily as the middle of a cartwheel, and their trousers are dirtied (ragged) at the bottom and their dickies (shirt fronts) about the colour of a marigold (yellow) and as many rings on their fingers as would make a dog-chain. I would not give a scalding of crabs (the smallest trifle) for a whole kennel-full of such like whelps.

II.

Come home to your children and me (Waugh).

1. I've just mended the fire with a cob,
   Old Swaddle has brought your new shoes.
   There are some nice bacon collops on the hob,
   And a quart of ale posset in the oven:
   I've brought your top-coat, do you know,
   For the rain's coming down very persistently
   And the hearth-stone's as white as new snow
   Come home to your children and me.

2. When I put little Sally to bed,
   She cried (be)cause here father wasn't there;
   So I kissed the little thing and I said,
   You'd bring her a ribbon from the fair;
   And I gave her a doll and some rags,
   And a nice little white cotton ball;
   And I kissed her again; but she said
   That she wanted to kiss you and all.

3. And Dick, too, I had such work with him
   Before I could get him up stairs;
   You told him, you'd bring him a drum,

ī sed wen īə͡ʳ sē-in iz prɔ͡ʳz
đen ī lūkt i mi fēs ən i sed
ast boɡə͡ʳts tēn aud ə mi dad
ən ī kraid til iz īn wə͡ʳ kwəit red
ī ləiks đi som (sụm) wīl dez jon lad

4. *ət lụŋg leŋgþ o git əm lē͡id stil*
ən ā͡ʳknt fọ̄ks fit ət went bəi
so o əiə͡ʳnt ọ mi tlūəz rīt wīl
ən o aŋgd əm oþmē͡idn tə drəi
wen od mendid đi stokinz ən šə͡ʳts
o sit dẹun tə nit i mi tšīə͡ʳ
ən o rēli did fīl rē͡idə͡ʳ ə͡ʳt
mon om ōnli wen đẹu ā͡ʳtnə dīə͡ʳ.

5. *ov ə drom ən ə trompit fə͡ʳ Dik*
ov ə jā͡ʳd ə blụu ribin fə͡ʳ Sal
or a buk ful ə bubz ən ə stik
ən som bakə ən pəips fə͡ʳ misél
ov braut đi ə njū kap tə-dē͡i
but o ọ̄ləz briŋgz sumət fə͡ʳ đi
ov braut đi som kofi ən tē͡i
in del fīl i mi pokit, đel sī.

6. *God bles đi mi lās; ol ɡə wom*
ən ol kis đi ən tšildə͡ʳ ọ rẹund
đa nọ̄z əz wīərevə͡ʳ o rọ̄m
om fē͡in tə get bak tə þuud grẹund
okn dū wi ə kruk ọ̄r ə dlās
okn dū wi ə bit əv ə sprī
but ov nọ̄ grē͡idli komfə͡ʳt mi lās
eksep wi jon tšildə͡ʳ ən đī.

He said when he was saying his prayers;
Then he looked in my face and he said:
Have the boggarts (evil spirits) taken hold of my dad?
And he cried till his eyes were quite red,
He likes you very well, does yon lad.

4. At the long length (= at last) I got them laid still
And I hearkened (to) the folk's feet that went by;
So I ironed all my clothes right well,
And I hanged them on the maiden to dry;
When I mended your stockings and shirts,
I sat down to knit in my chair;
And I really did feel rather hurt,
Man, I am lonely when you are not there.

5. I' ve a drum and a trumpet for Dick;
I' ve a yard of blue ribbon for Sal,
I' ve a book full of pictures and a stick
And some tobacco and pipes for myself;
I' ve brought you some coffee and tea,
If you 'll feel in my pocket, you 'll see;
And I've brought you a new cap to-day
But I always bring something for thee (you).

6. God bless you, my lass; I 'll go home,
And I 'll kiss you and the children all round;
You know that wherever I roam,
I'm glad to get back to old ground;
I can do with a crack (joke) over a glass,
I can do with a bit of a spree;
But I've no real comfort my lass,
Except with yon children and thee (you).

Index to Part. I (Phonology pp. 6 – 108).

Note: The words appear in their NE. forms except when there is no word in lit. English corresponding to the dialect word in form; they are then printed in italics in the ME. form. The numbers refer to the pages on which the words occur.

because 82, 103.
beds 94.
bee 31.
beech 30.
beef 33, 72, 85.
been 32.
before 8, 41, 42, 73, 85.
begin 104.
behave 108.
behind 92, 108.
behold 41, 70.
belch 96.
belder 15.
belief 86.
believe 32.
bellows 58, 95.
belong 22, 57.
bench 96, 98.
beneath 93, 98.
bent 53, 59.
be-out 8,
bequeathe 103.
bere-tūn 16.
berry 9, 100.
besom 95.
better 15, 59, 89.
between 98.
beverage 15, 59, 77.
beyond 92.
Bible 39.
bier 35, 57.
big 60.
biggen 18.
biker 18.
bile 38, 69.
bind 38.
bir 20, 63, 68.
bird 6, 17, 60, 101.
birlen 20, 63, 68.
bishop 96.
bitch 97.
black 11.
bladder 91.
blade 26, 70.
blame 27, 99.

bleach 97.
bleed 30.
blended 92.
blew 51, 71.
blind 17, 92.
blinken 18, 60.
blob 21.
blood 8, 54, 62, 84, 91, 99.
blot 21.
blow 49, 50, 67.
blue 51, 71.
boast 40.
boat 40, 87, 90.
bob 22, 61.
bobbin 21.
body 84, 91.
boglen 22.
boil (sb) 38.
boil (vb) 8, 52, 74. 84.
boisterous 52.
bold 41, 56, 99.
bolster 23, 56.
bolt 23, 56, 90, 99.
bone 40.
book 43, 62, 84.
books 94.
boot 90.
booth 93.
born 42, 57, 66.
borrow 100.
bosom 54, 88.
both 40, 93.
bottle 81, 103.
bottom 21.
bough 44, 71, 105.
bought 50, 70.
boulder 25, 67.
bound (adj) 92, 98.
bound (vb) 23, 44, 71.
boundary 44.
bow (sb) 50, 66.
bow (vb) 43.
bower 44, 75.
bowl 23, 70.
boy 52, 72.

braces 95.
branch 48, 61, 66, 96, 100.
brandnew 91.
brass 11.
brat 12, 58.
brazen 9. 13, 98.
bread 27.
break 36, 64.
breakfast 36, 65.
breast, 53, 59.
breath 34.
breathe 10, 34, 72, 92.
breeches 30.
breed 30, 72.
brew 51, 68.
bride 38.
bridge 18, 97.
bridle 91.
bright 20, 57, 65, 104.
brindle (up) 17.
bring 100.
broach 40, 67.
brodden 22.
broil 52.
brook 43, 103.
broom 42, 67.
brok 21.
broken 9, 54, 61.
brother 54, 93.
brought 50, 105.
brow 7, 43.
brown 43.
bulge 24, 61, 104.
bull 23.
bullock 78.
bunden 92.
bundle 24, 25, 62.
buoy 53, 72.
burlen 25.
burn 101.
burst 6, 11, 21, 60, 90, 101.
burre 25, 56, 63, 68.
bury 20, 59.

bush 96.
bushel 9, 96.
busy 18, 60.
but 84, 90.
butcher 79, 96.
butter 23, 61.
butterfly 76.
buy 38.
buzzard 24.

C.

cabbage 97.
cage 27.
cake 26.
calf 7, 13, 56, 66, 85, 99, 102.
calke 13.
call 13, 66, 67, 100.
calm 99.
cammid 12, 58.
can 14, 98, 102.
candle 91.
cang 12, 13, 58.
cap 11.
care 101.
careless 27.
carry 12, 100.
cartridge 97.
carve 16, 63, 101.
case 27.
castle 11, 77.
catalogue 80.
catch 12, 58.
cats 94.
cattle 79.
caudle 14, 79.
cause 48.
cease 30, 65.
certain 9, 17, 63, 81, 94.
chafe 85.
chaffer 12, 58.
chain 47, 55, 60, 72, 96, 98.
chair 47.
chalk 96.

champion 12, 48, 83.
chance 14, 48, 59, 96.
change 48, 96.
chap 12, 58, 96.
chapman 12.
cheap 27, 53, 59, 83.
cheek 31.
cheer 34, 57.
cheese 10, 95.
chemise 94.
cherry 94.
chest 18, 60, 90.
chew 51.
chief 32, 65.
child 8, 17, 74, 92.
children 91, 101.
chime 37, 69.
chimney 81.
chit 19.
choice 52.
choir 34, 57.
chosen 21.
chough 105.
Christ 38.
christen 7.
Christmas 76, 89.
chuffe 24.
churn 16, 68.
cinder 91.
clack 12.
clad 12.
claim 46, 71.
clay 46, 71.
clean 28, 53, 59, 71, 99, 103.
clear 34, 99.
clem 15.
clemmen 103.
climb 37, 84.
climbed 21.
clinken 18, 60.
clock 103.
clod 21.
close 41.
cloth 103.
clothes 40, 94.

cloud 43, 92, 103.
clout 43.
cloven 21.
club 84.
cluck 21.
clue 51.
cnorre 22.
coal 40, 41, 72, 78.
coat 8, 40, 41, 73.
coc 21.
cockle 103.
cod 21.
coffin 85.
coin 52.
cold 8, 9, 91, 99, 102.
colok 22.
colop 21.
colour 80, 99.
colt 23, 99.
column 98.
comb 54, 84.
come 7, 9, 23. 24, 61, 62. 88.
comfort 25, 61, 78, 85.
comical 22, 61.
coming 78.
commence 15.
company 76, 80, 88.
complain 46.
conceit 22, 61.
concern 17.
conny 14.
conquer 107.
consequence 108.
constable 79.
converse 17.
convert 17, 22.
cook 43.
cool 42, 100.
cop 21.
copper 21.
coral 22, 63.
cord 22, 66.
corn 22, 56, 68, 101.
coroner 55, 62.

costrelle 22.
couch 44, 71.
cough 50.
counsel 81, 95.
count 44, 98.
countess 77.
county 44.
cow 43.
coward 44, 76.
cower 44, 75.
coy 52.
crab 11, 84.
crabbed 92.
crack 11.
craft 85.
cramp 24.
cranky 13.
cratchinge 12.
creature 89, 102.
creep 9, 31, 72, 100, 102.
crept 7.
crib 17.
crikke 19.
crinkle 19, 92.
croft 21, 60.
crooked 103.
crop 21.
crow 50, 66.
crown 44, 100.
cruel 45, 73, 79, 99.
cruelty 79.
crumb 55, 62.
crust 24, 90.
crutch 24, 61.
cry 39.
crystal 76.
culter 25, 56, 67.
cup 84.
cup-board 23, 61, 83.
curd 101.
curds 24, 61.
curfew 82.
curse 9.
curtain 80, 89, 107.
cushion 96, 103.

custard 76.
cutten + leg 89.
cwic 17, 60.

D.

dab 13.
daft 11, 58.
dairy 47, 69.
daisy 46, 71.
damage 12, 58, 88.
damn 98.
dance 48, 69. 90.
danger 48, 97.
dank 107.
dare 14, 56, 90.
dark 16, 63.
darn 16, 68.
dash 14, 58, 96.
daughter 8, 50, 70, 90.
day 46, 47, 66, 90.
days 94.
dazed 92.
dead 27.
deaf 27, 71.
deal 28, 90, 100.
dear 83.
death 27.
debate 27.
deceit 77.
deceive 29, 64, 77.
deed 35.
deep 31, 65, 83.
deer 33.
defend 15, 85.
defy 85.
degen 15, 59.
degree 33, 65.
delay 46.
delf 85.
delight 39, 69, 77, 99.
deliver 82.
delph 15.
delve 15.
deny 39.

of 85.
offal 21.
offer 8, 85.
often 89.
oil 52.
ointment 52.
old 8, 41, 92.
once 41, 90.
one 41.
open 21, 54, 61, 98.
opened 92.
opinion 78.
orange 81, 97.
orchard 22.
ort 22, 56, 66.
ossen 22, 61.
ostrich 97.
other 54, 61.
ounce 44.
our 8, 101.
out 43.
oven 86, 98.
over 42, 73, 86.
owl 43.
owlet 55.
own, 50, 66.
oyster 52.

P.

pain 47.
paint 47.
pair 47, 69.
palace 79.
palm 13.
paper 13, 83.
parish 12, 58.
particular 80.
partridge 89.
paschen 14, 69.
passed 92.
passenger 98.
passion 13.
pasture 81, 89.
path 83, 93.
patient 95.
pay 46.

pea 94.
peace 29, 47, 83.
pear 36, 57, 69, 71.
pebble 83.
peg 104.
penny 83, 98.
pennyworth 78, 82, 87.
pens 94.
people 33, 72.
perch 8, 16.
pew 46.
pheasant 53, 59, 90. 95, 101.
philosopher 101.
pick 7.
pickles 103.
picture 102.
piece 32.
pier 33, 72.
pikin 19.
pint 39, 69.
pipe 37.
pismire 19.
piss-a-bed 19.
place 27, 99.
plain 47, 66.
plank 14, 61.
play 46, 83, 99.
plead 29, 65.
please 29, 53, 55, 60, 72, 95.
pleasure 53, 59, 95.
plecke 16.
plenty 79.
plough 44, 105.
plum 55.
plump 24, 62.
point 52.
poison 52.
poll 23, 70.
pool 42.
poor 43, 73, 86.
poplar 83.
posset 22.
pot 83.

potato 89.
pound 9, 23, 43, 83.
powder 91.
power 44, 75.
praise 95.
pray 47.
preach 29, 64, 97.
preserve 17.
price 39, 69, 100.
pride 38, 69.
priest 100.
primrose 19.
principal 76.
prison 95.
private 39.
promise 80.
proud 83.
prove 42.
provender 22.
prudence 45.
puck 55, 62.
pudding 83.
puff 24.
puffen 61.
pull 25, 67.
punch 24.
punish 26, 62, 78.
pure 83.
purge 20, 63, 68.
purple 77, 83, 101.
pursue 46.
put 83, 90.

Q.

quake 103.
quality 103.
qualmish 103.
quarrelling 77.
quarter 103.
queen 98, 103.
question 102, 103.
quick 103.
quiet 38, 103.
quilt 103.
quire 34, 74.

R.

radish 78.
rafter 12, 58.
rag 12, 103.
rail 47.
rain 46, 100.
raisin 80.
ram 14, 57, 61, 38.
rank 14, 57.
rash 14.
raspberry 83.
raven 26, 70.
raw 48, 66.
reach 28.
read 100.
ready 53, 59.
reason 29, 53, 70, 72, 100.
receipt 29.
receive 29, 33, 72.
red 53.
refuse 45, 95.
regular 80.
rehearse 108.
rein 47.
rejoice 52.
religion 97.
require 103.
resign 39.
rib 84.
ribbon 19.
rich 100.
riddle 35, 60, 77, 94.
ride 37, 100.
ridge 97.
rift 18.
rigge 18.
right 20, 65, 104.
rinele 18.
ring 100, 106.
rippen 18.
riven 18.
river 79, 86, 100.
road 40, 42.
roar 41.
roast 41, 73, 75.

10

rochet 22.
roggen 21.
roket 61.
Roman 81.
roof 42, 100.
room 9, 45, 88, 100.
root 42, 100.
rop 21.
rose 40, 73.
rough 55, 57, 105.
round 8, 44, 98, 100.
rout 44.
row (vb) 49, 67.
rub 8.
ruck 24.
ruckelen 24.
rude 45.
rue 51.
ruin 8, 73.
rule 51.
rupture 102.
rye 38.

S.

safe 49, 57, 64.
said 55, 60.
sail 46.
salt 13, 94.
same 26.
sand 94.
sausage 95, 98.
savage 49, 57, 59, 79.
save 49, 57, 71.
saw 48.
say 46.
says 55, 60.
scab 103.
scarce 103.
school 42.
schocken 22.
scissors 19, 95.
scoperell 21.
Scripture 102.
scrog 22.
scruff 90.

scum 55, 62.
scunneren 24.
scurf 23, 101, 103.
scythe 37.
sea 28, 64, 65.
seal 30, 72.
seam 28.
search 17.
season 29.
sedge 97.
see 31.
seed 35, 65.
seek 30, 97.
seemed 92.
seize 29.
separate 76.
September 83.
serke 16.
sermon 17.
serpent 17.
servant 17, 81.
serve 17, 101.
seven 86.
shade 26, 70.
shadow 9, 82, 87, 96.
shame 13.
shanks 21.
sharp 84, 101.
shear 36, 57.
sheep 34.
sheet 32, 65.
sheriff 85.
shift 18.
shilling 7, 8, 107.
shine 37.
shipp 96.
ships 9, 94.
shire 39, 74.
shirt 20.
shoe 42.
shone 41.
short 96.
should 99.
shoulder 25, 56, 60.
show 51.
shower 44, 75.

shove 55, 62, 86.
shred 53.
shrew 51, 68.
shroud 43, 100.
shunt 24.
shut 24, 25, 61, 96.
shuttle 20, 25.
sib 18.
sick 32, 60.
sickle 103.
side 37.
sight 20, 104.
sign 38.
silent 39.
silly 77, 78.
simple 9, 19, 83, 88.
since 18.
sind 19.
sing 9, 18.
singer 106.
sink 107.
sissen 19.
sixth 6, 18.
size 95.
sker 16, 68.
sky 39.
slash 14, 69.
slaughter 49, 105.
sledge 16.
sleep 34, 72, 99.
sleeve 32, 72.
slide 18.
slink 18.
slough 57, 105.
slow 50, 66.
slut 24 61.
slutch 24.
small 18.
small-pox 95.
smash 14.
smell (vb) 88.
smithy 18.
smoke (sb) 40.
smooth 42, 93.
smother 88.
smothered 92.

snake 26.
snekke 16.
sniff 90.
snizen 19.
snout 98.
snow 50, 67, 98.
so 40, 87.
soap 40, 41.
soften 89.
soil 8, 52, 72.
sold 41, 70.
soldier 102.
sole 55, 70.
solid 92.
some 25.
somebody 23, 25, 61, 78, 91.
somewhat 23, 82.
song 23.
soon 42.
soot 43.
sop 21.
sore 41.
sorrow 100.
sorry 41.
sought 50.
soul 50, 70, 100.
south 43.
sow 44, 50, 71.
spade 26.
span 14.
spare 27.
sparrow 83.
speak 36, 64, 83, 94.
spear 36.
special 33, 64, 79, 95.
speech 35, 64.
speed 30, 72.
spew 51, 68.
spider 94.
spink 18.
spirit 19, 20, 59, 83.
spite 38.
spitel 18.
spoil 52.

spoken 54.
spoon 42, 73.
spread 28, 100.
squire 39, 74.
stair 89.
stairs 47, 57, 69.
stand 14.
staple 26.
star 101.
stare 27, 68.
start 16, 63.
starve 16.
station 95.
steak 47.
steal 35, 36, 100.
steam 28.
steel 34.
steep 28, 65.
steeple 32, 65.
stile 38, 69.
stink 9, 107.
stir 20.
stirk 20.
stood 54, 62.
stool 42, 100.
stone 40, 94.
stoop 45.
strange 48, 61, 97, 98.
stranger 97.
straw 89.
stream 28.
street 34, 100.
strength 107.
strife 38, 85, 100.
strike 37.
strive 38.
strong 23, 106.
stronger 106.
struck 22.
stubble 24, 77.
study 26, 61.
stump 25.
succeed 33.
such 6, 18, 87.
suck 55.

sudden 81.
suet 8, 73.
sugar 45, 62, 95.
suit 46, 67.
sum 24, 62.
sup 55.
sure 101.
swaddle 94.
swallow (vb) 82.
swallowing 106.
swan 14.
swap 87.
swear 8, 9, 36.
sweat 28, 61.
sweet 30, 77, 87.
swelten 87.
swilling 106.
swim 88.
swine 37.
sword 87.
sworn 42.
swot 87.
syllable 19.
syrup 19, 59, 78.

T.

take 9, 13, 103.
tale 26, 70, 89, 100.
talk 13, 99.
taper 26.
tarried 92.
teach 28, 64.
tear (sb) 30.
tear (vb) 36.
teeth 30.
tell 100.
tempt 83.
tenten 15, 16.
terrible 16, 63.
terrified 104.
that 93.
thaw 48, 66, 92.
theatre 8, 32, 72, 101.
thee 31, 93.
their 47, 69, 93.

then 93.
there 93.
þerf 16.
they 47, 93.
thief 31, 65, 85, 92.
thimble 38, 60, 84.
thine 93.
thing 106.
think 18.
third 18, 20.
thirty 20, 63.
this 10, 93.
thong 87, 93.
thorn 22, 68, 92.
those 40, 41, 93.
thou 44, 93.
though 105.
thought 50, 105.
thousand 44, 92.
thread 34.
threat 53.
thrive 39, 69.
throat 40.
throng 23.
through 23, 105.
throstle 21, 89.
throw 50.
thrush 25, 58, 61.
thumb 55, 84, 88, 92.
thunder 7, 10, 23, 92.
thwack 93.
thwart 93.
thwittle 19.
þwyten 93.
tick 19.
tickle 19.
tie 32, 38, 74.
tiffen 90.
tiger 39.
tile 38, 69.
timber 84.
time 37, 88, 89.
tīnen 38, 65.
tip 19.
tit 19.

tithe 38.
titten 19.
toad 41.
toast 41.
tobacco 82.
toddle 21.
toe 40.
toil (vb) 52.
token 54.
told 41.
toll 23, 55.
tomb 45.
to-morrow 100.
tongs 23.
tongue 89.
too 42.
took 43.
tool 42.
tooth 42, 73, 93.
tough 50, 57, 105.
toward 82, 92.
towel 81.
tower 44, 89, 101.
town 8, 9, 44, 89.
toy 53.
trample 14.
travel 81.
tread 35, 36, 72.
treasure 80, 95.
treat 29, 47, 64.
tree 100.
tremble 19, 84.
trestle 16.
trindil 18.
trollin 21.
trough 50, 57, 105.
truce 95.
trumpet 25.
trundle 24, 91.
truth 51, 71, 93.
tumble 84.
tune 102.
tunne 23.
twelve 85.
twine 87.
twinkle 87, 103.

10*

Table of Contents.

Part II: Accidence.

Lebenslauf.

Am 16. März 1867 wurde ich, Karl Georg Schilling, evangelischer Konfession, als Sohn des Schuldirektors Georg Wilhelm Schilling zu Altrincham in der Grafschaft Cheshire, England, geboren. Bis zu meinem 15. Jahre besuchte ich meines Vaters Schule, später ßing ich nach der Manchester Grammar School. Im Jahre 1884 bezog ich das Aberystwyth College der Universität Wales und wurde im Jahre 1886 an der Universität London immatrikuliert. Im Jahre 1902 wurde ich als Lektor des Englischen an der Universität Giessen bestellt, wo ich zur Zeit tätig bin. Zu gleicher Zeit habe ich vom Oktober 1902 bis zum August 1905 an der Universität Giessen studiert. Vorlesungen habe ich während meiner Studienzeit besucht bei den verehrten Professoren und Dozenten Prof. Dr. O. Behaghel, Prof. Dr. Behrens, Prof. Dr. W. Horn, Lektor Goetschy und Lektor Thomas. Ihnen allen spreche ich an dieser Stelle meinen Dank aus. Zu ganz besonderem Dank bin ich Herrn Prof. Dr. W. Horn verpflichtet, der mich zu meiner Dissertation angeregt und mir stets mit seinem Rat zur Seite gestanden hat.

Lightning Source UK Ltd.
Milton Keynes UK
UKHW010631151121
393997UK00001B/124

9 789353 897895